FINDING YOUR VOICE

A Path to Healing for Survivors of Abuse

MANNETTE MORGAN

Mad
PUBL

D0377683

Made For Success Publishing
P.O. Box 1775 Issaquah, WA 98027
www.MadeForSuccessPublishing.com

Distributed by Made for Success

Publishing Library of Congress Cataloging-in-Publication data

Morgan, Mannette

FINDING YOUR VOICE:
A Path to Recovery for Survivors of Abuse
p. cm.

ISBN: 978-1-64146-374-4 (PBK)
ISBN: 978-1-64146-396-6 (HDBK)
ISBN: 978-1-64146-375-1 (EBK)
ISBN: 978-1-64146-445-1 (ABK)
LCCN: 2019939285

I dedicate this book to the following:

Thank you, Mom, for always unconditionally loving, supporting, and believing in me. You have always been my rock as well as my sounding board, no matter what choices I made.

I am grateful to my husband who supported me throughout this daunting seven-year journey as I spent most of my time in solitude, putting my thoughts, beliefs, and experiences on paper. Thank you for your support and patience, which I realize is a lot for you to give. It did not go unnoticed.

Thank you to my daughter and son, who supported me sharing our personal challenges with the world for the greater good of humanity.

To my son, I appreciate and value how our relationship has evolved and grown into a powerful friendship along with your supportive encouragement and willingness to listen.

To my daughter, thank you for sticking with me years ago when I was merely surviving and learning how to be a better mom. I know I made mistakes, but you have always been a remarkable young lady with unwavering confidence and strength. Your support and friendship mean more to me than you will ever know.

I am so proud of both of you and the incredible adults you have become.

Thank you, Kate, for listening and debating my logic, bringing my attention to current events as I processed and explained every aspect of abuse that comes with the healing process. You're a wonderful friend and a remarkably intelligent individual.

And finally, thank you to Jen Clark, who taught me how to clearly define my words through coaching, editing, and lots of patience as I learned to express myself on these pages.

Thanks to everyone at Made For Success Publishing for helping me make this book a reality.

I couldn't have done this without any of you or your support.

Thank you,
Mannette

Contents

FINDING YOUR VOICE

Introduction

• • • • • • • • • • • • • • • • • • • •

I BELIEVE THE BOOK YOU HAVE IN YOUR HANDS will give you valuable insight, tools, and wisdom to help you navigate the healing process after surviving abuse. I want to speak to the survivors who have become overwhelmed by sadness and pain, who endured and lost all hope of ever being happy or feeling fulfilled. My wish is to give you hope so you can start lifting the heavy burden of abuse from your shoulders. Even if you've begun to work through your healing with a therapist or counselor, I hope this book will inspire you and help you discover a new way to start healing your past. Healing is a personal journey without any time restraints. This book is designed so you can work at your own pace as you dig deeper into the healing process.

Most of us wait until we feel as if we are drowning in desperation and hopelessness before we consider changing our lives and seeking answers. When we find ourselves completely pulled into the current of pain, we finally realize we need to grab hold of something to stay afloat and eventually pull ourselves out of the water. However, if we don't reach out for someone or something, we could find ourselves sinking. My friend, thank you for reaching out and grabbing hold of this book. I believe it can be a valuable piece of your personal healing process.

Though I don't know your story or where you are in your journey, I want you to have the opportunity to heal from the inside out. I am not a doctor or therapist; I'm a woman just like you who somehow found a way to survive abuse. I'm a woman who decided I didn't want to be a victim anymore. I'm a mother who knew in my heart there was something better for my children and me. I'm a person who decided I wanted to change my life, and now I'm a woman who wants to share what I have learned with you. Some of my words may feel intense, and you may not be able to get them out of your mind. If I may be so bold, maybe that's your cue that it's time to start listening so you can start healing.

This book is only one person's view of how to heal after abuse, and I don't expect that you will agree with everything you read. I feel strongly that you should form your own ideas and opinions about everything – not simply take something as truth because someone else said it. Only you know the details of the things you've experienced, and every person's journey is different. There is no right or wrong way to heal after abuse. The beauty of this is if you are reading this book with the desire to heal, you can't mess it up, and you are moving in a more positive direction. Though each story is unique, there are millions of us working on this healing thing, and you are not walking through your journey alone.

As you go through this book, I will be sharing details about *my own* experience. I want to let you know before you start reading that I respect each and every person's choices about religion, spirituality, and personal beliefs. Each individual's story is an intimate, personal experience. My intention is simply to help you heal in any way you can.

I want to tell you upfront that this journey could be the rollercoaster ride of a lifetime. I'm not going to tell you this ride will be easy, but I will tell you that this ride can help you transform your life as you know it. This ride will teach you things about yourself you never knew existed while helping you discover the person you were born to be. I suggest you hang on tight as you navigate the twists and turns of newfound joy and hope until you're ready to lift your hands into the air and feel the wind rushing through your hair as you exuberantly come alive again.

How This Book Works

I have designed this book to take you on a journey of self-exploration. This includes examining your thoughts, beliefs, and behaviors. I will ask you to inquire, probe, and analyze yourself with personal, enlightening questions. I will provide activities and exercises to help you deal with the challenges you will face while making changes in your life. I have also provided some samples of my own personal experiences throughout the book. Each example is designed to help you understand and relate to different subjects.

My intention is to help you learn how to understand more about yourself as you progress through the healing process. You might want to consider getting the *Finding Your Voice* Workbook to document your answers, exercises, and activities as you go along. The companion *Finding Your Voice* Workbook can be a great tool if you need structure and guidance. As you go through this book, I suggest flagging or highlighting particular subjects to provide a quick reference source for you to revisit.

Other helpful items in this book include exercises, questions, and affirmations. You will find scaling questions throughout the book, which can be a good tool to evaluate where you started and how far you have come. You may want to revisit some of these scaling questions once you finish the book, along with some exercises. You might be surprised how differently you respond to some of the questions by the end of the book.

There is no right or wrong answer to any of the questions asked throughout the book. Each question is an opportunity for you to learn more about how you feel, who you are, and what you want. This is your own personal journey of healing, and no one else's. All I ask is for you to proceed without judgment and try to remain open and honest with yourself. Here are a few scaling questions to get you started.

Introduction Questions: (1 being not at all, 10 being extremely in alignment with the topic or statement.)

How happy are you with your life?

1   2   3   4   5   6   7   8   9   10

How happy are you with yourself?

1   2   3   4   5   6   7   8   9   10

My Awakening

• • • • • • • • • • • • • • • • • • •

SITTING ON MY VERANDA, I'm lost in thought as the gently ring-
ing wind chimes dance in the crisp, late summer breeze. Time
seems to stop while I gaze at the mountain behind my amazing home
through the 60-foot pine trees. When a hummingbird buzzes by my
head, the sleeping puppies at my feet start to stir, unmoved for the
next several minutes. I think of how far I've come from that dilapidated, blue and white trailer house on a Texas ranch. I recall the green
carpet that disguised patches of mold growing along the backside of
the living room and the musty fragrance on any muggy, summer day.

I left the ranch at 18 when I moved
to a suburb of Dallas to live with
my high school sweetheart. Years
later, I found myself in Western
Colorado with my third husband.
Soon after that, we moved to
Singapore, traveled around Asia,
and experienced the exotic sights

and smells of different cultures, and met expats from all corners of the world. Four years later, when I arrived back in the Rocky Mountains, I knew I was home for the first time in my life. Today, I live in these beautiful mountains with my loving husband and two crazy schnauzers in an immense home filled with warmth and love.

Each one of us has a story, and no two stories are the same. This story is just one of thousands of stories out there waiting to be told, and this story happens to be mine.

As a young girl, you could find me riding my buckskin horse Pokey, with my long dark hair flowing behind me just like Pokey's tail. Most of the time, I would be screaming, "Whoa, Pokey! Whoa!" as he ran away full speed down the old dirt road adjacent to my grandparents' old farmhouse. I was the only girl and the oldest of three. My loving mother was a rancher, just like her dad and his parents before him.

Our days on the ranch were full of hard work taking care of cattle, horses, the garden and the occasional pig or goat. My brothers, mom, and I helped my grandmother take care of my chronically ill grandfather, playing dominos most afternoons in the smoke-filled farmhouse, eating my grandmother's baked cookies. Every afternoon my brother and I walked back down the driveway to our old, dilapidated, blue and white trailer house. When dad came home from work, our small house went silent as we all made ourselves scarce, never knowing what kind of state dad would be in. My brothers and I were like the wild rabbits on the ranch – fragile and jumpy, always hiding – only we hid from our dad instead of coyotes.

I was a child who learned how to survive my ever-changing emotionally abusive environment. My dad was a brilliant, eccentric engineer. He was a fearless entrepreneur who was also emotionally detached and full of rage. My dad's words could leave much deeper wounds than the belt he occasionally used on us. For all his brilliance, he knew nothing about raising us kids. He was unaware of the emotional damage he inflicted on my mother, brothers, and me. My dad had to survive his own childhood abuse and neglect, the product of his own emotionally unstable mother and alcoholic father. So, the cycle of abuse and alcoholism continued with us.

Within my rural world, I only knew my caring, creative mom and my hardworking, unstable dad, along with my kind, God-fearing grandmother, ill grandfather, and a modest, sometimes judgmental community. I learned to pay close attention, stay out of the way, and become invisible. Despite my extroverted, optimistic, and free-spirited nature, the real me slowly faded away.

I was unaware of the world outside the ranch, other than our weekly Friday night trip to Dallas for a dinner out. As we drove, I looked out the truck window, longing to live among the bustle and lights of the big city. Most days, when I wasn't helping on the farm, I would sit quietly on my small bed, scanning the pages of the National Geographic magazines, desperately trying to read the captions, wanting to travel the world and understand the difference between people and cultures. Thank goodness pictures say a thousand words since I couldn't read. I was unaware that I had a learning disability, just as I was unaware of my family dysfunction.

I couldn't see that my childhood was preparing me to be the perfect victim, ready for my next abuser. I was an innocent, naïve, skinny eight-year-old girl. I never imagined that I should be fearful of my older cousin until the day he became the ultimate monster. It was

3

like he had been ready and waiting for the perfect moment to step up and claim me as his prey. Before I realized what had happened, my abuse wasn't just emotional anymore – it had turned into a nightmare of physical and sexual abuse.

My cousin lived on the farm across the creek with his parents. Once my nightmare started, I tried desperately to avoid him, but he was smart and manipulative. He was the oldest grandchild and everyone thought he was responsible and protective of all of us younger kids. No one knew he was the monster that lived among us.

His smell turned my stomach, and the hay caused tiny irritations on my soft skin. The old barn across from my house was his location of choice to probe and violate my body. He persistently tried to convince me that I was inciting and inviting his sexual behaviors, but inside I knew it wasn't true! I spent every night alone in the dark, kneeling down on my knees, praying to God to make him stop, but God didn't hear my cries. I began to believe that God had forgotten me, or He had decided I was the dirty little girl my cousin told me I was. For nearly five years, my perpetrator exploited my body and manipulated my mind while I suffered in silence and held on to my horrifying secret. Gradually, I went from frightened, confused and fighting, to numb, disconnected, and submissive. By the time he was done with me, I was internally lost, shattered, and broken.

After years of surviving my cousin's abuse, I was finally freed from his grasp. Over the next few years, I didn't need my cousin to actively torture me to continue living in the nightmare he'd built, my torture continued in the form of PTSD (Post Traumatic Stress Disorder) and OCD (Obsessive Compulsive Disorder). I became an overachiever in every aspect of my life – from social school activities to my personal appearance.

I continued to cope with my experience and my learning disability (dyslexia) while overcompensating for all of my insecurities. At fifteen, I was primed and ready to take on my next abuser. This time, he came in the form of a handsome football star with blond hair and an unbelievable smile. I couldn't imagine what he saw in me. I was just a stupid girl with a disgusting secret. I believed I was damaged goods and undeserving of love. He swept in, and before I knew it, I was playing the role of the victim once more.

This abuse was different, and it came in the form of gaslighting and narcissistic behavior. One minute he would tell me he loved me, and the next he was criticizing how I looked, along with everything I did or said. He had a special way of making me believe he loved me while convincing me that I didn't understand his sarcastic, cruel humor, and adamantly reinforced that everything was my fault. Then he would proceed to tell me I was overly-sensitive. I lived in a constant state of heightened emotions from "love" to heartache. Of course, I chose to participate in this abuse. My part was to serve myself up on a silver platter for him to devour without hesitation. The whole victim role was all too familiar and seemed normal to me, even if I was always suffering. No one understood why I stayed with him, not even me.

I played this degrading victim role for almost ten more years as he continually dished out the abuse, always expressing how I deserved the abuse he supplied. Then, I found myself at 23 years old with two beautiful children; my youngest was only one year old. One morning, I saw myself reflected in a person on a television talk show, the depressed victim striving to become a survivor. There I was – crying out of desperation while hiding from the world. My optimism and the happy mask I wore shielded me from the truth, from myself, and from years of deep-seated pain. I could finally see the truth that I was a victim who needed to become a survivor. If not, one day I might look up when I'm 50 and find myself living in an old trailer house showing my daughter how to be a victim and my son how to be an abuser.

For the first time in my life, I began to face my fears, step out of denial and choose to seek out help, not only for me but for the health and wellbeing of my children. Once I sought out knowledge, I was able to see the unhealthy dysfunction in my life clearly. The moment I opened my eyes and saw the truth, I left my husband and started my personal healing journey.

My healing journey hasn't been easy; in fact, it felt like a roller coaster of emotions, with dramatic ups and downs, occasional abrupt stops, along with reliving the pain from my past and the challenges of my present life. No matter how crazy the ride, I was determined to change my life and eventually heal my wounds.

In the beginning, I felt alone, and at times, it was overwhelmingly dark. In time, I could see the light and felt hope in my heart. As I healed, I discovered my value, inner-strength and eventually, my self-confidence. I learned to let go of the shame and to forgive the little girl that survived her horrific childhood, as well as the young woman I became. As a young mother, I began to take responsibility for my choices and the life I had created after abuse. I learned to accept and love myself for the survivor I became unconditionally. For the first time in my life, my insides started matching my outsides, and my smile became more authentic as I learned to express all of my emotions – the good, the bad and the ugly. I guess you could say I found myself, and I let the real me shine for the world to see, with grace and gratitude for the life I've had as well as the life I'm creating.

I finally experienced compassionate love, along with respect from another person, and his name was David. I felt I was the luckiest woman in the world. He treated me like the loveable, respectable person I was, which was uncomfortable at first, but eventually, I learned to accept his love along with his kindness. We had a loving, healthy relationship for ten years that helped me grow, heal, and learn my worth in a transformative way. He was my biggest fan and supporter, along with my mother, until the day he died.

At that point in my life, I had acquired healthy boundaries and had mended certain family ties, while letting go of old relationships that didn't serve me well. I finally learned how to cultivate healthy relationships. I had created a successful business, a beautiful home, and a healthy life for me and my children. Little did I know there would be more challenges and the roller coaster ride would continue, but this time with fewer extreme turns, fewer stops, without abuse and intermingled with times of joy. As time passed, I could take on anything that crossed my path, and I knew I would be okay.

My husband Luke walked out on the veranda, shaking me from my thoughts and back to the present moment, enjoying the sun beaming down across my beautiful mountains. I took stock in it all.

What I Know Today

Today I'm lucky, and I enjoy the company of my husband, children, family, and friends. I have come a long way mentally, and emotionally. I breathe in each day with gratitude and a desire to learn something new about myself and the world. I no longer need drama or chaos in my life. I made a choice years ago to let go of guilt, shame, worry, and most of all, fear. I'm at peace with my past, present, and future – whatever that might be. I unconditionally accept, love, and respect myself, as well as others. I understand that my thoughts, along with my actions, have manifested the life I have today. I follow my dreams and desires as I embrace more joy and happiness in my life. This is where I am today, but this isn't where I started 27 years ago.

What kind of life do you want to live?

How I Got Here

You can achieve the life you want to live, just like I did. When I was 23, I didn't know my life could be any other way. But I cultivated a dream of something different for myself and my children, even though initially the dream was vague. At that point in my life, I thought everyone could see my insecurities, lack of confidence and despair. I believed I was damaged and unworthy of love, much less respect. I couldn't see that not all relationships were chaotic and unpredictable. I even believed most men were uncaring and manipulative. I was wrong.

I devoted myself to a year of group therapy and four years of individual therapy. I immersed myself in the self-help realm, learning about abuse and its repercussions. I dedicated myself to changing my life, healing my pain and forgiving myself. I have spent the last 30 years on self-care (being kind, gentle, loving, and compassionate to myself) and have ultimately achieved my dream of a healthy and happy life.

Here is a list of my "truths" developed over the three decades I have spent working on my healing.

- I understand that I will make mistakes and fall down, which is perfectly okay.

- I allow myself to feel deeply, with honesty, while being true to myself.

- I have a choice to apologize and rectify my mistakes.

- I can choose to be present each moment of each day.

- I have a choice to do my best and my best is enough.

- I can choose to reflect and learn from my misfortunes and challenges.

- I have a choice to forgive myself and others.

- I have a choice to get up, try again or do something different.

- I can choose to find tolerance, acceptance and love for others who are different or challenging.

- I can choose to see past the petty things that don't deserve a reaction or a response.

- I choose to love and accept myself and the world without conditions.

- I choose to respect myself and the world along with everyone in it.

- I choose to treat myself with kindness.

- I choose to be resilient and optimistic.

- I choose to accept my life with grace.

- And finally, I know everything is as it should be, and all is right in my life and the world. No matter what has happened in my past.

My Wish

I have written this book for all the women in the world that have been abused, assaulted, degraded, dismissed, lost, scared, confused, judged, or left hopeless. I want you to know you are not alone, and there is hope for you as well as your children. My wish for you is that you learn from my experiences and knowledge so you can stop suffering and begin healing.

You are the director of your life and the creator of your future. You possess the power to change your life for the better. You can heal and live a life with hope, love, joy and happiness. You are a gift to yourself and this world!

CHAPTER 2

Cultivate Your Healing Tree

• • • • • • • • • • • • • • • • • • •

YEARS AGO, MY THERAPIST shared a valuable book with me called *The Courage to Heal,* written by Ellen Bass and Laura Davis. Working through this book was a challenging task for me, and I struggled to comprehend some of the information. My dyslexia made things even more difficult, as I still labored to read with my limited vocabulary.

After I had moved through all of the different challenging stages of healing, I wanted to simplify and organize the healing process for survivors, so they could make small, lasting changes to help restore their lives to fullness. I decided to create a tree metaphor along with the diagram below to represent the various stages of healing and how these stages can influence your life and your experience.

The diagram represents five stages of healing from abuse. After years of therapy and intense self-reflection and work, I believe these five stages are the most concise way to make necessary changes to heal after surviving abuse. Walking through these stages of healing can be challenging and emotional, but I assure you, it can be done.

5-Blossoms (Leaves)
Embrace
Happiness
& Joy

4-Branches
Discover Yourself

3-Trunk = BAR
Behaviors, Actions &
Reactions

2-Roots = The Big 3
Unconditional Acceptance,
Love & Self-Respect

1-Seedling → Step Out of Denial

Fifth Stage: Flowers and Leaves
Discovering Happiness and Joy

Fourth Stage: Branches
Discovering Yourself

Third Stage: Trunk
Behaviors, Actions & Reactions

Second Stage: Roots
Embrace Unconditional Acceptance, Love & Self-Respect

First Stage: Seedling
Stepping Out of Denial

If we think of ourselves as seedlings, the first thing we must find is a great location to plant ourselves, so we can grow and thrive. Maybe you'll choose to be a mighty oak tree in a beautiful, quiet meadow near a small stream if you are the kind of person that loves tranquility and solitude. Or maybe you would choose to be a magnificent blue spruce, wedged between two strong, sturdy rocks on a mountainside with lots of other evergreens or aspens if you are the kind of person that wants more adventure and enjoys the company of others.

Whichever type of person you imagine yourself to be, once you are planted, you will likely find yourself desperate for water and sunlight. As you feed on these nutrients and start to grow, you will eventually push your way through the soil into the light. This looks a lot like stepping out of denial and accepting the truth of your abuse so you can seek help.

Before you know it, you will grow into a baby tree, bearing a few baby leaves. By this point, your roots have started reaching deep into the earth. These roots represent your foundation, which I believe is the relationship you have with yourself. This includes learning how to accept and love yourself unconditionally and growing in self-respect. As time goes on, you will see how important it is to have a strong foundation to support your tree as well as your beliefs.

As you continue to grow, your trunk will become more rigid. This process mirrors the way you react to challenging situations, developing specific behaviors and habits. You are constantly changing, just like the weather. Some storms are challenging, presenting themselves with wind, hail, and snow, while others pass by with a gentle breeze. Even still, you have the ability to face each storm and season in stride: your trunk is strong and immovable.

After weathering a few storms, your branches start to reach out toward the sky and over the landscape. Just as your branches reach out, as you heal, you will start to reach out for your needs, wants, and desires. As you discover more about yourself along with your desires, those branches will become resilient and sturdy as you face future storms.

Finally, you will start to blossom through the tips of your limbs with flowers and leaves. Now that you're aware of your needs, wants and desires, your flowers and leaves represent the joy and happiness you are seeking. Perhaps your leaves are bright green or your flowers fragrant as you shine for the world to see.

Remember, you are on a journey of healing, and that journey doesn't happen overnight. Be patient, face each challenge one at a time, and focus on the things that stir up emotion within you or speak deeply to your heart. One day you will be able to look up and know you have faced your past with dignity and healed one wound at a time as you work your way through the stages of healing.

Let's keep moving forward together and start healing your life.

CHAPTER 3

Is It Real?

•••••••••••••

"When you are a small seedling in the dense, dark forest of life, it can be hard to see the forest much less the light."

I WAS A 24-YEAR-OLD, young, insecure mother of two children. My oldest was a precious three-year-old boy, with blond hair and blue eyes like his dad, and my youngest, a one-year-old girl with dark brown hair and brown eyes exactly like me. At that point in my life, I was a wife, a mother, and the owner of a small interior design business. Everything in my life was moving along as I thought it should; my life seemed normal to me. I occasionally felt sad, empty, and lonely; I had felt that way most of my life. I thought everyone felt that way. I was a caring mother and wanted the best for my children, but I often felt disconnected from them. I also felt indifferent with family, friends, and my husband most of the time. On the outside, I wore a smile, and I appeared to be happy while in control. On the inside, I felt empty and alone.

One cold winter morning, while I was cleaning my house, I noticed a guest on a morning talk show talking about depression. They started explaining the symptoms of depression: sadness, loneliness and helplessness. I couldn't believe it — they were describing me and how I had felt for years.

I started to grasp the fact that I had become a great actress in order to survive and cope through the years. I was a pro at putting on my happy face, taking care of everyone else, and being the strong one. I had learned to be whomever and whatever I needed to be in any situation. All I ever truly wanted was to be a good person. However, I knew in my heart something had been wrong for a long time, and that something now had a name: depression.

Can You Recognize Abuse?

You are most likely holding this book because you or someone who cares about you suspects that something isn't right in your life. Maybe someone shared this book with you because they can see the pain you live with or that your heart is broken.

Can you conceive that something could be wrong in your life and that you might need help?

I intend to help you understand the in-depth layers of abuse and how it can impact your life. Would you recognize abuse if you saw, heard, or felt it? Abuse isn't just rape, incest, or physical attack. Abuse comes in all forms, ranging from verbal and emotional maltreatment to physical violence.

Let's start with your relationships. Are any of your relationships disappointing or full of drama? Do you let others control or dominate your life? Are your relationships built on lies and deceit? These are signs of unhealthy relationships that could point to some form of abuse. I want to help you understand abuse and all the different ways it can look, sound, or feel.

Below are statements and questions for you to contemplate. I want you to ask yourself if they relate to any part of your past or present life. The only thing I ask is for you to be honest and truthful with yourself. I believe healing starts with honesty and self-awareness.

 REFLECTIONS

Do these statements sound like you or someone you know? Take out your workbook and put a check by the statements you have experienced.

- I don't know why I choose to have relationships with people who take advantage of me.

- I don't understand why I can't take care of myself or others.

- I put everyone else's needs before my own.

- Why is there always so much drama in my life?

- I don't know why my family or friends have so much drama in their lives.

- I don't understand why I'm betrayed by the people I care about.

- Why do I push people away who are nice and kind to me?

- I don't know why I choose to have relationships with people that hurt me.

- I don't know why I lie to people.

- I don't know why I'm always afraid of what people might do or say to me.

- I don't know why I'm always trying to overachieve or strive for perfection.

- I don't understand why I tend to have an addictive personality.

- I'm never satisfied and always want more. (This can include love, attention, animals, food, alcohol, clothes, jewelry, etc.)

- I don't know why I put myself in harm's way.

- I don't understand why I feel so disconnected from everyone else in the world.

- Why do I lack certain emotions in my life such as joy, love, pleasure, anger, or sadness?

- I don't know why I feel numb most of the time.

- I don't understand why I'm angry so often.

- I don't know why I feel guilty, embarrassed and apologetic for everything that happens, even if I'm not at fault.

- I don't know why I have this deep-rooted feeling that I'm not enough, no matter what I do.

- I don't know why I feel I deserve less than anyone else even when I tell myself I can do or have anything; I never truly believe myself.

Are you surprised by how many statements resonate with you? Don't worry, we all have to start somewhere. I'm going to help you work through the process of denial, acceptance and understanding.

The statements above illustrate how we perceive ourselves after experiencing abuse. Most of the statements focus on how we feel about ourselves, while others focus on how we perceive and participate in our relationships. We acquire specific beliefs and behaviors – as well as survival and coping skills – during and after experiencing abuse.

I believe if you relate to a majority of the statements above, you may have experienced some type of abuse or neglect in your life. The following definitions should help you understand if this applies to your life.

Definitions of Abuse

Abuse: Any action that intentionally harms or injures another person.

Verbal Abuse: A form of psychological/emotional abuse consisting of the use of abusive and demeaning language with a spouse, child or elder, often by a caregiver or other person in a position of power. Examples of verbal abuse include name calling, belittling, derogatory and critical remarks.

Psychological Abuse: It includes threatening the victim with violence, harassing them when they are outside the home (E.g., at school or work), denying the victim access to others (E.g., refusing to allow the victim to see friends, preventing use of the telephone), confining the victim to home, or destroying the victim's property. It is often difficult to prove. Can also be referred to as psychological violence, emotional abuse, mental abuse or gas-lighting. Examples of psychological abuse are emotional/mental manipulation, control, and passive-aggressive behaviors.

Physical Abuse: Any action that intentionally harms or injures another person. Physical abuse can happen to both children and adults of either gender and any sexual orientation. The injuries can be inflicted by punching, kicking, biting, burning, beating, or use of a weapon such as a baseball bat or knife. Physical abuse can result in bruises, burns, poisoning, broken bones and internal hemorrhages.

Domestic Violence: Intentionally inflicted injury perpetrated by and on family members; varieties include spouse abuse, child abuse, and sexual abuse, including incest. Examples of domestic violence can be physical, sexual, emotional, psychological actions or threats of actions that influence another person. This can include using economic domination or control over another person.

Sexual Abuse of a Child: Sexual behavior between an adult and child or between two children, one of whom is forcefully dominant or significantly older. Sexual behaviors can include touching breasts, genitals, and buttocks while the victim is either dressed or undressed. Sexual abuse behavior also includes exhibitionism, cunnilingus, fellatio, or penetration of the vagina or anus with sexual organs or objects. Pornographic photography also is a form of sexual abuse of children.

Sexual Assault: The forcible perpetration of an act of sexual contact on the body of another person, male or female, without his or her consent. Legal criteria vary among different communities.

Rape: Sexual intercourse (vaginal or anal penetration) against the will and without the consent of the individual.

Incest: Sexual activity between persons so closely related that marriage between them is legally or culturally prohibited.

Now that you are more aware of the different types of abuse, let's go a little deeper and see how these definitions relate to you and your relationships. Below are some questions that reflect patterns and behaviors that can be abusive. The next sets of questions are designed to help you recognize if you are living in an abusive situation or not. Not all abusive situations are the same, just like not all relationships or people are the same. If you are questioning your current or a past relationship, I have provided a website that can help you better understand specific types of abuse.[1]

I refer to your partner in each question, but this can also include a spouse, parent, guardian, relative, friend, or authority figure. Such authority figures could include a stepfather, grandparent or teacher,

---

1. https://www.helpguide.org/articles/abuse/domestic-violence-and-abuse.html

as well as immediate family members. The following question can apply to your past or present life:

Monsters or Lambs

Are the people you have relationships with monsters or lambs? Take out your workbook and put a check by the questions you answer, "Yes."

- Do you feel your partner controls you?
- Do you feel your partner controls your relationship?
- Does your partner try to make you feel guilty?
- Does your partner force or guilt you into having sex or engaging in sexual acts with no regard for what you want?
- Does your partner insult, discourage or say cruel and hurtful things to you?
- Does your partner tell you that you can't make it without them while implying you aren't good enough?
- Does your partner seem like they have two different personalities, one personality in private and one personality in public (a Dr. Jekyll and Mr. Hyde personality)?
- Has your partner ever said, "I wouldn't have to do that or act that way if you wouldn't push my buttons or act like you do?", after they have hurt you?
- Does your partner have unrealistic expectations for what your role is in the relationship or do they change those expectations frequently?

- Does your partner try to isolate you from friends or family?
- Is your partner cruel to animals or children?
- Does your partner have unrealistic expectations for animals or children?
- Have you endured any physical, verbal, emotional or sexual abuse in any of your past or current relationships?
- Have your children been physically, verbally or emotionally abused by anyone?

Note: If you or your children are in danger, please get help as soon as you can so you can find a way out of your monstrous situation.

If you answered "Yes" to any of these questions above, or if you have experienced any of the definitions above, **start getting help now!** Please physically remove yourself as soon as possible from any situations where you may still experience abuse; this can include family members, friends, and acquaintances or partners. If you are in an abusive relationship, seek out help from a therapist, domestic violence group, an organization for abuse, local authorities or someone you can trust. Once the situation escalates, the time for taking a "wait and see" approach is over. It's time to consider other options to protect and take care of yourself and your family. I have listed a few organizations and hotlines on my website *Mannettemorgan.com* and in the reference portion of this book.[2]

---

2. The National Coalition Against Domestic Violence (NCADV): https://ncadv.org/resources

The next set of questions will help you recognize if you are flirting with a relationship that could become abusive. We call relationships that could become abusive 'borderline abusive relationships.' I feel it is best to be aware of what kind of relationships you are involved in, so you can make healthier decisions for yourself.

Borderline Abusive Relationships

If you answer "Yes" to one or more of the questions below, you could be in a relationship that has the potential to be abusive. It's best to keep your eyes and mind open while being true to yourself, especially if you have experienced abuse sometime throughout your life.

- Is your partner overtly jealous, and does the jealousy seem to increase the longer you are together, without cause?

- Does your partner blame others for their problems or shortcomings?

- Is your partner hypersensitive, easily insulted or always feeling as if others are attacking them?

- Do you act differently around your partner than you do with friends or family? Do you find yourself hiding things from your partner? Do you find yourself hiding things from your friends or family that happen in your relationship?

- Are you more emotional when your partner isn't around?

- Are you a different person when you have a break from your partner?

- Do you feel safer and more relaxed when your partner isn't around?

- Do you ever fear your partner?

- Do you ever have suicidal thoughts because of your relationship? If so, please get help by reaching out to National Suicide Prevention Lifeline: 1-800-273-8255.

All of these questions are designed to help you see the truth in your own life, so you can get help to change your situation. If you have trouble acknowledging that what happened to you was real, much less abuse, take a moment and give yourself permission to accept the truth. You may have grown up in a family that dismissed your abuse as experimental, acceptable, or even untrue. Some of you may only remember fragments of your childhood, but those fragments are painful. You may have haunting memories that something terrible happened; you just don't have a clear picture of what transpired.

Some of you may feel like you put yourself in a relationship or situation that turned out dangerous. On the other hand, some of you have a clear understanding of your abuse and feel like you have dealt with it, only to find it is still haunting you today. Whatever place you find yourself, it's time to step out of denial and into acceptance so you can start healing.

Do you believe you are worthy of being helped? If the answer isn't a resounding "Yes" I'm here to tell you, yes, you are worthy of being helped – no matter what you think about yourself. No one deserves to be abused. We are all worthy of having healthy relationships, no matter who we are or where we come from.

Unfortunately, I personally experienced most of these different types of abuse above from childhood throughout my first marriage. The first time I asked myself some of the questions above, I was stunned by the answers I gave. As a 24-year-old wife, I couldn't believe I was in an abusive relationship. Once I realized it, I was terrified of what I needed to do, which was to **get help, get out, and start over.** This decision and action are not going to be easy, but you are worth it and so are your children, if you have them. Please step out of denial into reality and understand that no matter how hard it seems, you do have a choice to take back your life and stop living with abuse.

1. **Get Help:** I started by assembling a support system of trustworthy family, friends and a professional therapist. My therapist helped me understand the abuse I had experienced throughout my life. This helped rebuild my confidence and strength to prepare for the next step.

2. **Get Out:** I made a plan to get out of my abusive relationship. I got a lawyer and filed for divorce with the support of my parents and continued my therapy.

3. **Start Over:** I had to learn how to take care of myself, so I could start building my new healthy life as a single mom. You may not realize it right away, but you have the capacity to do the same.

"When you're ready to see the truth,
someone will show you the way."

Put on Your Glasses and See Reality: Step Out of Denial

When you are ready to see your truth, someone will show you the way. I didn't know I was ready to see my truth until one defining morning while watching that talk show. In the beginning, it was easier to deny the truth than accept that abuse had molded and shaped every aspect of my life and my relationships. I even questioned whether anything was really wrong or not. People around me tried to tell me that nothing was wrong, and they knew what was best for me. Be wary of those people—they could be trying to prevent you from seeing the truth, or they could just be fearful of you changing. You have a right to seek out a healthy and happy life, don't let anyone tell you any different.

"When the student is ready, the teacher will appear."
BUDDHIST PROVERB

The morning I heard the talk show giving me a definition of depression, I felt like I was the ready student for whom the teacher had just appeared. I knew I needed to do something. I've always been a take-charge, fix-it kind of person – at least once I understand there is something to fix. I didn't have the luxury of the internet back then to look up information about depression or abuse, but I did have a resource. Through my husband's work, there was a limited therapy program for the employees and their families. It seemed so easy! I'll go to a therapist for eight or nine weeks, get better and move on with my life. I had no idea what was ahead. I found a therapy group and went through the phone interview process. Afterward, my head was swimming with questions and self-doubt. Did I really have a problem? Was all of this as bad as it seemed? Maybe I'm imagining all of this, and it isn't actually a big deal? Somehow, even after the interview, I found the courage to make the appointment.

I wanted to hear what the therapist had to say. In the beginning, there was a part of me that constantly questioned myself and the decision to seek help. Who am I to take time and money to do this for myself? Is there anything even wrong with me? Maybe all of this is just in my head. However, once I started the process, I realized I did need help, and I had quite a few things to work out, both in my past and present life.

So that was when my journey of healing began. Looking back, it's easy to see that the show and the interview with the therapy group were "teachers" appearing in my life, letting me know it was my time to choose to become a student. I put on my backpack and went back to school to learn about abuse, healing and most of all, myself. It was the first time in my life that I started taking care of me.

My first appointment was with a male therapist who immediately told me he couldn't work with me. He explained to me that I needed to see a female therapist who specialized in childhood sexual abuse. Soon after I started working with a female therapist, I quickly realized this process might take more than eight or nine weeks. Once I realized how my childhood sexual abuse had affected my life up to this point, I was determined to get through the process as fast as possible. I also began to realize how my past abuse could affect my children's well-being and future. My therapist helped me understand that the statistical probability of some form of abuse happening to my children was almost inevitable if I didn't work hard to change the patterns and stop the cycle.

Even when I wanted to give up, I knew I had to continue therapy. No matter how hard or emotional it was for me, all I wanted to do was mark this particular task off my to-do list and move on – just like I had done after every traumatic experience I endured. Little did I know, this wasn't something I would mark off quickly. I did the work and rode the emotional roller coaster for quite some time. I wasn't about to give up, even if this was the hardest thing I had ever done.

For the first time in my life, I was learning to take care of myself first, and I realized I deserved to be free from any type of abuse. The teacher had appeared, and my eyes were open. I could finally see the truth and how the abuse had shaped my life.

The Costumes of Abuse Survivors

After experiencing abuse, there is always some similarity of symptoms or characteristics. Some of us deal with depression, anxiety or even addiction. I can sometimes recognize these symptoms or emotions when I meet someone that has experienced some kind of abuse. It can be as simple as overcompensating for their insecurities, to an unequivocal sheepish demeanor. We all have telltale signs after our experiences with abuse. What costumes do you wear?

It's important to have a baseline for feelings and behaviors you've experienced throughout your life. You may have felt one or more of the following emotions: shame, insecurity, disconnection, depression, helplessness, hopelessness, joylessness, unworthiness, confusion, anxiety, insanity, anger or judgment. You might feel out of control and overly critical of yourself and others. Do any of the following resonate with you? Have you acquired any of these emotions or behaviors?

You may have experienced one or more of the following:

- Intentional or unintentional self-abuse, destructive behaviors, eating disorders, alcoholism, drug abuse, or addiction. You may have even put yourself in dangerous situations or unhealthy relationships.

- Erratic behaviors and inconsistencies in your boundaries, communication and interactions with others.

- Erratic behaviors or inconsistencies in your parenting skills when teaching, disciplining, interacting with, or communicating with your children.

- Feeling unsupported or cast out by your family or different friends throughout the years.

- Abusive tendencies toward your family or children.

Have you experienced any of these destructive behaviors? Which ones?

Have you experienced any of these situations in your life? Which ones?

Learn How to Walk, Then Run

You're a survivor now; you're not the victim anymore. As you move through the many stages of healing, know that there is no formula. You might move through some stages gracefully, and others you may revisit over and over again. Some of the stages may be quite painful and overwhelmingly emotional. Remember, you are on a journey of healing, and every journey has its ups and downs. Be kind to yourself as you navigate through this process.

Your journey of healing is all about baby steps. When a baby is learning to walk, the journey starts with crawling, then standing while holding onto something stable, then stumbling and finally walking. It's the same for you as you learn to accept that your abuse was real and begin to explore how it affected your life. You will learn to crawl through the trauma, stand on your own while finding your balance, then begin to walk. Occasionally, you will fall, and you may even feel like you are going backward. It will be okay. It's all part of the process. We all have to push ourselves to move forward – just like a baby learning to walk.

Asking for and Receiving Help

It is time to start asking for help, even if it is incredibly hard. Seeking help is one of the first steps to a healthier life. After surviving abuse, some of us don't feel we are deserving of help. Ladies let me tell you: *everyone* needs support. Everyone. Even Superwoman!

You may want to seek out professional help from a therapist, counselor, or psychologist that specializes in abuse. Group therapy for survivors of abuse or an abuse recovery support group can be another good alternative. I feel it is also beneficial to have a good personal support system that includes friends and family you can trust. It's important that these people can listen with compassion and without judgment. You may want a few different people to help offset the load they are helping you carry. A support system is vital as you progress through the healing process, and a safe place to vent is a gift.

You may even need some alone time to process your emotions. You might need a sitter for your children so you can take time out for yourself and spend time on your emotional health. You might consider a solo trip to help you clear your mind and encourage new, healthy behaviors.

As you start making changes, it can benefit you greatly to ask people you trust and respect for their advice and opinions. Two brains are better than one, especially when you are learning new behaviors and attempting to produce a new action or response to a given situation. It's also good to evaluate your thoughts and opinions with people you trust. Just as you would get a second opinion from a doctor, getting a second opinion from a trusted friend will help you see something you may have never seen before.

One of the most courageous things you can do throughout your healing process is to find someone to share your journey with. Before you start the conversation, it's important to clarify what you need from the other person. This might be expressing that all you need from them is to listen and provide a safe place for you to share, not advice. You might say that you are not asking them to express their opinion or give you constructive feedback; you are just asking them to be supportive and non-judgmental while you share your experiences. Most importantly, make sure you feel safe and secure with the person you choose to share with.

After stepping out of denial and leaving my abusive situation, asking for help was the next hardest thing for me to do. As is the case with most, it was hard for me to believe I was worthy of anything, much less help from a professional, friend, or family. I eventually had to ask for and receive their support, even if I didn't like it. I want to let you know you are worthy of being helped; we all are. The challenge that comes with asking is that we may have been taught to believe we are less than, and that is completely false.

I remember the day my therapist handed me that little yellow brochure for a survivor's group, that explained how abuse could change people's personalities. I couldn't believe the information I was reading. All I could say to myself was, "That's me. That's me! Oh my god! That is why I'm the way I am." I had struggled for years and often wondered why I reacted to certain situations the way I did. I also didn't understand why I chose to do things that caused me pain and drama. I didn't like conflict and wouldn't stand up for myself in most of my relationships. I always put everyone else's needs before my own and went so far as never to take care of my own needs. I would never say no to anyone. When I was forced to say no, I always felt a tremendous amount of guilt. I had always been remorseful for every situation, no matter if I was at fault or not. I always lived in a constant state of fear and often wondered, what am I so afraid of? Even after my childhood abuse had ended.

I attended a group for survivors of incest and sexual abuse once a week for months, and it was a great experience. The group helped me understand how different people react and cope after abuse. No two people deal with the repercussions of abuse the same way.

It took me some time, but I realized that my eyes were opened, and I could see the darkness for what it was: a dysfunctional life because of abuse. I had been a victim, and now, it was time to be a survivor. It was a wake-up call for me personally, and the first step to help me understand why I acted the way I did and why I seemed to attract the same types of relationships. I could hardly believe that most of my behaviors were repercussions of abuse. I was previously unaware that I had accepted a false self-belief that I was not worthy and that I was less than everyone, especially the people closest to me.

This brochure and group were a gift that changed my life and my views. It helped me understand what happens to victims, their personality, and their behaviors after abuse.

Stop the Cycle

I firmly believe that sharing your story, especially with your family, is crucial to stopping the cycle of abuse. We can't stop abuse if we choose not to recognize it. It is preferable to share your story with a supportive family member. Some families create an environment that allows the abuse to be passed down from generation to generation. Most families don't even realize how the cycle of abuse has developed within a family and how it can grow like cancer. This might be in part because family members choose to keep abuse secret. They choose to look the other way or don't accept that the abuse has happened. Some people wind up with no support system and no one within the family that believes them. Sometimes the family knows the truth yet refuses to support the victim.

In many families, the victim is isolated and disrespected. They are forced to sweep the abuse under the rug and expected to move on in silence. I truly feel sorry for these victims because not only are they violated by the perpetrator, they are also abandoned by the people who should have protected them. To me, this can sometimes be worse than the abuse itself. Not only have they experienced abuse, but they aren't given support, security, respect, or their voice. This situation makes it quite difficult for these victims ever to trust or feel respected in their relationships. If this is your story, you may need to build major boundaries in your existing relationships with immediate or extended family. Then you can replace those unhealthy relationships with healthier ones.

The following are a few statistics on abuse from the National Association of Adult Survivors of Child Abuse (NAASCA) website, and the numbers are astonishing:

- It is conservatively believed that today one in four girls and one in six boys will be sexually molested before they are 18 years old.

- Somewhere between 2/3 and 90% of sexual abuse victims never tell!

- 90% are abused by someone they know, love or trust.

- 60% of American children are exposed to violence, crime, or abuse in their homes, schools and communities.

- Children exposed to violence are more likely to abuse drugs and alcohol, suffer from depression, anxiety, and PTSD, fail or have difficulty in school, and become delinquent and engage in criminal behavior.

- One in five teen girls and one in ten teen boys are victims of dating violence.

- 1 in 4 women and 1 in 9 men will experience domestic violence in their lifetime.[3]

It's time to reach out and ask someone to help you out of your unhealthy life. Try not to be afraid of the unknown; it's probably better than what you have had to face up to this point. You can do it. I know you can.

Emerging Out of the Darkness

I could finally see that I was a seedling that couldn't see through the dense forest of my situation without help. I was small and needed help to grow, and I didn't have to do it alone. I had a choice to reach for my share of the sunlight and nutrients just like every other tree; I just had to step out of denial and choose to try something different than I had before.

Now that you are starting to recognize abuse and all its forms, you can also step out of denial and see your truth. It is time to realize you are not alone, and there are millions of us out here. You have a choice to free yourself from your past and the pain of your secrets while finding your voice. Hopefully, you know by now that you

---

3. http://www.naasca.org/2012-Resources/010812-StaisticsOfChildAbuse.html

don't have to do this alone. This is the biggest and scariest step you will take, and I'm going to be here with you every step of the way. You have to choose to accept the truth and move forward one baby step at a time until you eventually learn how to walk and then run.

Follow-Up Questions

Am I in an abusive relationship?

Have I been in an abusive relationship?

Did I grow up in an abusive situation?

Do I know what type of abusive relationships I've experienced?

Am I ready to help myself?

Can I accept that I'm not Superwoman and I need support?

Can I see that I'm worthy of help?

Am I ready to learn how to live a healthier life?

Have I ever been to counseling or therapy for my abuse? If not, why?

What is it going take for me to get the help I need?

CHAPTER 4

The Roots of Your Life

• • • • • • • • • • • • • • • • • •

I STILL REMEMBER TO THIS day how I felt as that little girl. I was scared, sad, trapped, and all alone in my horrifying world of abuse. I remember wondering, how did I get here? How did this happen, and what have I done? He was a great manipulator and convinced me that I had caused this horrible thing to happen. He convinced me that I was simply an undeserving little girl that no one would believe or protect. I knew I hated what he did to me no matter what he said.

I spent years praying to God, asking him to stop my abuse, only to be disappointed again and again. As a little girl, I felt ashamed for the abuse I was experiencing while deeply hating myself for the situation I thought I had created. I would cry, I would fight back and I would pray, but none of it made him stop. I bartered with my abuser and God for almost five years before I finally found a way out of the horrifying situation.

By the time I was a teenager, I only saw my imperfections, and I hated both my body and the person living inside. I often would hide in my closet late at night, sticking my long fingernails into my upper inner thighs until they would bleed and bruise as I cried. I longed for my damaged outsides to match my painful inside, feeling so out of place and unworthy of love. I despised the way I carried my shameful secret with a smile on my face. Loving myself was the furthest thing from my mind. In fact, I was in my mid-twenties before I realized I didn't have to be a victim anymore. I could be a survivor. It took years for me to learn how to find compassion for the little girl who suffered abuse. It took even longer for me to reprogram my old negative thoughts as a young woman.

> *"Embrace the strong, confident individual*
> *you were always meant to be."*

Let's start with nurturing our seedlings. The best place to start is with our roots, which are essential for our foundation. The foundation I'm talking about in this context is the relationship you have with yourself. This relationship is all about acceptance, unconditional love and self-respect, which are what I call *The Big 3*.

The journey to healing and finding new strength begins with *The Big 3*, or your root system. Deep roots come from an ability to accept yourself no matter what. They will continue to grow as you learn to love yourself as you are – imperfections and all. They will grow deeper as you learn how to respect yourself while recognizing all your amazing abilities and qualities. Below I have listed both the definitions for *The Big 3* as well as the opposite definitions so you can identify how you feel about yourself currently.

The Big 3

1) Acceptance: The act of being received as adequate or suitable; regarded with favor or approval for oneself.	**Criticism:** The expression of disapproval of someone or something based on perceived faults or mistakes
2) Unconditional Love: A strong affection for another or yourself; affection based on admiration and kindness without conditions.	**Conditional Love:** Affection and kindness based on conditions; love that exists within certain parameters.
3) Self-Respect: Pride and confidence in one's self and a feeling that one is behaving with honor and dignity.	**Disrespect:** Lower regard or esteem for someone or something. An expression of disapproval; to hold in contempt.

Be honest: can you say you unconditionally accept, love, and respect yourself just the way you are?

If you were abused as a child, you more than likely learned guilt, shame, fear, worthlessness and even subconscious self-loathing. Victims of childhood abuse usually find it difficult to learn how to love themselves unconditionally as they mature. Survivors of abuse also find it hard to accept that they deserve love or respect from others, especially from the people they love.

As you embrace *The Big 3*, you will be astounded at how much greatness you begin to see in yourself.

You cannot change what happened, but you *can* choose to start healing. Why not start by learning to love yourself well? A good start is to ask yourself, "How do I want to start living my life for myself?"

Everyone deserves to live a life free of abuse, experiencing joy and peace in their everyday lives. One of the most valuable insights my therapist shared with me was that I had to choose to learn to love myself. She said, "You have to love yourself first. If you don't choose to love yourself, how can you honestly receive love from someone else?" In other words, if I didn't learn how to accept, love, and respect myself, no one else would either.

How can you expect your children, family or partner to love or respect you if you don't love or respect yourself?

I want you to get in touch with how you perceive yourself today and in the past. Remember, there are no right or wrong answers to any of the questions I ask you throughout this book. Each question is an opportunity for you to learn more about yourself. This is your journey, and no one else's. Here are a few reflective questions. (The scaling questions have a base of 1, being not at all, 10, being extremely in alignment with the topic or statement.)

How much do I accept myself the way I am today?

    1   2   3   4   5   6   7   8   9   10

How critical am I of myself?

    1   2   3   4   5   6   7   8   9   10

How critical was my family growing up?

    1   2   3   4   5   6   7   8   9   10

How much do I unconditionally love myself?

    1   2   3   4   5   6   7   8   9   10

How often do I place conditions on myself?

    1   2   3   4   5   6   7   8   9   10

How conditional was love within my family growing up?

    1   2   3   4   5   6   7   8   9   10

How much do I treat myself with respect?

    1   2   3   4   5   6   7   8   9   10

How much do I treat myself with disrespect?

    1   2   3   4   5   6   7   8   9   10

How much disrespect was there within my home growing up?

    1   2   3   4   5   6   7   8   9   10

Now that you are starting to understand how you feel about yourself, I want to help you understand how you got here. None of us became hypercritical and self-bashing on our own; we learned these habits through our experiences and trauma (likely during early or late childhood). So how did your childhood shape *you*?

How Yesterday Shapes Today

I believe we are all a product of our inherent nature as well as what we learn as children from the people around us. Our childhood experiences shape our personality, behavior, beliefs and character. It is where we learn the foundation of either conditional or unconditional acceptance and love. It is also where we discover how to respect ourselves and others. Our childhood shapes the basis of our self-worth and how we perceive ourselves. If you grew up in a dysfunctional and abusive environment, you would most likely repeat those learned behaviors, either by abusing others or subjecting yourself to abuse.

Before the age of six or seven, most humans have discovered that there's a specific way to fit into their family. You have learned what emotions are acceptable (e.g., happiness, joy, love) and which are unacceptable (e.g., anger, sadness, fear). You have also learned if the love you receive from your parents has strings or conditions attached. Maybe you've been taught that you have to do well in school or be a great athlete to receive love. Maybe you were taught crying isn't acceptable or told, "I'll give you something to cry about," when you were upset.

By watching my mother with her parents and others that worked on the farm, I learned what unconditional acceptance, love and respect looked like. She was good to everyone she encountered. She was always kind and gracious, even when others weren't so kind to her. She taught me from a young age to always treat others the way you want to be treated and respect everyone for their abilities. On the flip side, I learned fear from my father. I learned how to stay clear of people with anger issues. I learned to pay attention to people's behaviors, and that some people have less control over their emotions than others. Unfortunately, I also learned to be complacent with people who have emotionally abusive tendencies, which is part of the reason I didn't tell anyone about my childhood sexual abuse. I didn't feel worthy of being protected. My childhood – just like yours – had both positive and negative circumstances that shaped me into the person I am today. Every experience was a lesson learned.

Get to Know Your Little Girl

I feel it's much easier to heal the person you are today if you choose to communicate and connect with the child within. This was one of the key factors that helped me heal from childhood sexual abuse, family alcoholism, and growing up with dyslexia. Looking back now, I wish I would have focused on this years ago. I had to learn how to show compassion and understanding for the child within me – the one who survived the abuse and other challenges I faced.

Some say childhood innocence always knows the truth, but only speaks if we are willing to listen. Maybe it is time to start listening as you allow your inner child to speak. If you feel lost when it comes to connecting with yourself, be assured you are not alone. Most of us have ignored and dismissed the inner child because we suffered deeply. Connecting with your inner child can be a wonderful healing experience. The more you learn to connect with your inner-child, the easier it is to understand where your childhood pain originated from and where you still carry it as an adult. The validation you give yourself by connecting with your inner-child can heal so many of your old wounds. As an adult, you can start nurturing and protecting your little girl once you acknowledge her.

I remember the first time I acknowledged Nena (little Mannette). I don't think she was ready to acknowledge me. I didn't even know how to start the conversation or what to say to her. It seemed so silly and ridiculous to talk to myself. Once I got over my fear, I finally took the plunge. One night before bed, I started openly talking to Nena. The first conversation I had with her was me babbling about something that happened that day, and I felt ridiculous!

As time went on, I learned to respect Nena for her insight into what she and I had been through as a child. It was really hard for me to open my heart and accept that she had suffered and never healed. Once I started listing to her, I realize she had been shut down from the time she was four or five years old. She wasn't allowed to be the outgoing, charismatic and inquisitive little girl she was always meant to be. I eventually learned how to tell Nena how much I loved her and how sorry I was for all of the things that happened to us throughout our childhood. We both learned to heal while moving through the pain, disappointment and loneliness of our lives. We slowly learned to respect and support each other. Now she is a healthy, happy little girl who truly loves life, and I'm a strong independent woman who has learned how to embrace life.

The following exercise can help you deal with old recurring challenges as well as things you want to rediscover about yourself. I suggest that you pace yourself as you move through, starting with the first step. Give yourself some time to process before moving on. The purpose of this is to reconnect with a part of yourself you may have abandoned or disconnected from to survive. Your inner-child can also hold the answers to your current beliefs and desires. Some people are reluctant to connect with their inner child, and you may find yourself a little terrified or anxious as you do so. I promise it is worth it!

The following are a few things you may want to consider before starting the exercise:

- Try to remember this little girl is you as a child. She may have been alone for years and felt totally abandoned and ashamed.

- Your inner child is the key to most of your pent-up emotions, including shame, fear, worry and anger.

- Remember to always be compassionate and kind to your inner child. She has endured a lot.

- It's time to be the big sister or mother your inner child needs (and may have never had). Your nurturing instinct will most likely tend to start protecting your inner child once you reconnect and recognize she is a part of you.

- Your inner child has been waiting for you for a long time, and you are strong enough now to care for her.

- Once you have made the connection, don't forget she is a part of you and always has been. While you grew up, she was stuck in time with all of her emotions.

Getting to Know Your Little Girl Exercise

Take out your workbook so you can document your answers and how you feel after doing the following exercises. Find a quiet, safe place where you will not be disturbed and make your space as comfortable as possible. Consider playing soft background music or lighting a candle or two – whatever it is that creates a calm and relaxing environment for your experience. If you have a childhood toy or object you love, hold it while you proceed with this exercise. If you have a picture of yourself at a young age, you can use it to re-familiarize yourself with that young child.

Step One:

You can sit up straight or lie down, whichever feels best for you. Close your eyes and slowly take three deep breaths, relaxing your mind and body.

Start by relaxing every part of your body as you breathe deeply, starting with your feet and legs. Now move slowly up through your hips and stomach. Next, I want you to relax your chest and arms. Finally, relax your neck and head.

Imagine a white, almost clear protective bubble surrounding you.

Step Two:

Once you feel safe and protected, start by picturing yourself when you were a little girl. It could be the little girl that experienced a diffi-cult situation or the little girl after she survived. Start a conversation and ask your inner child the questions below. The ultimate goal is to let her know you are ready to listen to her and her needs so you can start supporting her from now on. Remember to pause, closing your eyes and giving her time to respond throughout the process.

Statement and Questions for Reconnection:

Hello, little _____ (Fill in your name or nickname you were called as a child).

This is ___. (Fill in your name.)

I'm so sorry nobody protected you, and I have ignored you for so long.

I want you to know, I'm here for you now, we are safe and I love you with all my heart.

I'm really proud of you for everything you did to try to keep us safe years ago. I promise to treat you with love and compassion as we get to know one another again. I know we have been through a lot, but we will be okay. We have each other now.

Can we talk now? (Pause)

(If not, why?)

Can I at least talk to you, so we can build a better relationship? (Pause)

If you aren't feeling as if you are getting a response from her, continue to express how you feel about her while including positive things that she did. If you feel she is responding, continue with the following questions:

How are you doing? (Pause)

Is there anything you need from me? (Pause)

Is there anything you want to show or tell me? (Pause)

Now your job is to stop and listen. Listen inside your mind and be patient for answers.

She may not respond in a bold, loud voice; her response could be soft whispers or a knowing within your mind.

What does she sound like?
Is her voice timid and subdued, or loud and angry?
Can you see her?
What is she wearing?
Where is she?
Do you recognize anything around her?

Whatever you hear, see, smell or feel, accept it as truth and know that she is here with you. Don't dismiss her or turn her away. She is as real as you because she is you. She just needs to be respected and heard. Let her share how she feels without judgment. Let her connect with you while you become her best friend and protector.

Each time you do one of these exercises, be sure and thank her for opening up to you. Then take time to be kind to her and the woman you are today. This exercise will likely be an emotional and enlightening experience. Take it slow and be patient.

If you feel emotionally safe and ready to move forward, you can move on to step three and ask her a few more questions. If not, take a break and do this exercise another day after you have processed your emotions.

Note: You may want to flag this page, as you will come back to this reconnection exercise as we move forward throughout this book. You can go to Mannettemorgan.com for other tools and guided relaxation meditations to make this process easier.

Step Three:

Do you feel safer today than you did years ago? (Pause)

Are you still afraid?

Are you still in pain?

How can I help you heal?

Once you are done, tell her how much you love her and miss her. Then thank her for trusting you enough to share her thoughts and feelings. Slowly open your eyes and take a couple of deep, slow breaths.

Now I want you to give yourself a big hug. It took courage for you to open yourself up and have an honest conversation with your inner child.

Additional Techniques: If you are still struggling to connect with your inner child, here are a few more out-of-the-box ways to reconnect or use the exercise above.

- Get out your workbook and ask your inner child a question from the exercises above. Write down whatever comes to you. Don't think about it or worry about your spelling or punctuation, just write down whatever comes to you.

- Write down a question for your inner child from the steps above with your dominant hand and let your inner child answer by writing short answers with the non-dominant hand.

- Ask your inner child to draw a picture of how she feels. Let her express herself with art instead of words.

The idea is to let your inner child express herself in whatever way she can. It's important to always go with your first gut feeling or thought; try not to question whatever comes to you. Everyone has an inner knowing, so don't question what you feel, hear or see when you do these exercises. Remember, the purpose of this process is to help you understand your inner child so that you can heal your old wounds. This exercise isn't about guilt or regret; it's about healing.

Connecting with Your Little Girl

Connecting with your little girl is a continuation of sorts from step one. It's now time to ask your inner child how you formed your negative beliefs. As I've said before, most of our insecurities are formed at some point in our childhood and carried into our adult lives. If you struggle with feelings of insecurity, hatred, criticism and disrespect, it can usually be traced back to when you experienced those particular feelings as a child. If you understand where those insecure feelings originated, it can be easier to make a change, or simply let them go.

This next set of questions is designed to help you understand where and when these insecure beliefs originated. Once you know where they started, you can discover how factual these beliefs are. You may even discover that you acquired and absorbed the beliefs of others, so much so that you thought they were your own.

Here is a list of just a few of the challenging emotions you might deal with as an adult that might have formed in your childhood: guilt, shame, fear, worry, anger, sadness, resentment, self-criticism, self-hate, insecurity. Ask yourself the following questions so you can understand which emotions relate to you. Remember, none of the questions or exercises are meant to discourage you; they are intended to enlighten you.

List which insecurities apply to you.

Base Questions for Insecurities:

When was the first time I remember feeling unloved?

When was the first time I remember feeling inadequate?

When was the first time I remember feeling ignored?

When was the first time I remember feeling unappreciated?

When was the first time I remember feeling self-critical?

When was the first time I remember feeling ashamed?

When was the first time I remember feeling afraid?

When was the first time I remember feeling defensive or angry?

When was the first time I remember feeling less important than others?

Connecting with Your Little Girl Exercise

Recall Exercise:

You can sit up straight or lie down, whichever feels best for you. Once you are comfortable, repeat the reconnection exercise from the page you flagged. After you have reconnected and are feeling relaxed, I want you to ask yourself what insecurity you are feeling today. When you have it, try to remember the first time you experienced that particular emotion. Keep your workbook close by so you can document your answers.

Step One:

The following is an example, and you can replace the first question with any of the feelings from above (or ones I have not listed).

1. When was the first time I remember feeling unloved?

2. Where am I?

3. What is happening around me?

4. How old am I?

5. How do I feel about the situation?

6. Is there anyone else involved?

7. What are they doing or saying?

The intention is to become aware of how your insecure feelings and beliefs originated. Once you are aware of when and where a triggering event might have happened, you can look at who may have been involved and how you have replayed these feelings over and over again. After you have connected with the event and how you were feeling, it is important to follow up with the questions below. You might start remembering multiple events or emotions, but it is important to not take on every insecure feeling at once. Instead, only work on one to three things at a time. You can always come back to this exercise and deal with other insecure feelings or challenges later.

Step Two:

Write the following answers down in your workbook:

Is it true, or untrue?

Do I really believe it?

Why am I choosing to believe this belief?

Is this someone else's opinion or belief? (A parent, family member, or someone else?)

Am I owning someone else's belief? Why?

Was the situation as bad as I remember?

Does it matter to me now?

Am I still holding on to insecurity that doesn't even really apply to my current life? Why?

What will it take for me to let go of my past and live for the now?

Once you recognize your insecure feelings and beliefs from a different perspective, you might be able to discredit some of your old beliefs instantly. Now you can start to understand why you feel the way you do about yourself.

It might take some time for you to recognize how and when you got here. Give yourself grace. Keep in mind that healing starts with understanding, and that is the goal for now.

Hang in there; you're doing great.

"The little girl inside you knows your truth."

Discover What Your Little Girl Knows

Discovering what your little girl knows is all about discovering your personality or spirit that you may have once lost along the way. In most cases, there are some positive experiences we can remember from our childhood. Most of us received some kind of love, acceptance, or encouragement at some point in our childhood. Maybe your parents made you feel that you had to prove yourself constantly, but you had a teacher who saw the potential in you. Maybe your sister constantly bullied you, telling you that you were ugly, but your grandma reminded you of how beautiful you were inside and out. Your inner child always knows; the goal is simply to reclaim your empowerment.

The following questions are designed to help you remember the times you felt loved and accepted. Some of these questions might help you rediscover your value, as well as help you find more empowerment.

Take your workbook and write down your answers. If you don't remember or can't answer, don't worry, move on to the next one.

Base Questions for Acceptance and Love:

When was the first time I felt loved?

When was the first time I felt accepted?

When was the first time I felt pretty?

When was the first time I felt smart?

When was the first time I felt respected?

When was the first time I felt seen and heard?

When was the first time I felt appreciated?

When was the first time I felt important?

Discover What Your Little Girl Knows Exercise

Recall Exercise:

After you're in your comfortable, relaxed state, go back to the flagged page for the reconnection exercise. After you're connected, I want you to focus on the first time you experienced acceptance or love in your life. Just like with the previous exercise, I want you to ask yourself the following questions for each item.

For Example:

When was the first time I remember feeling loved?

Where am I?

What is happening around me?

How old am I?

How do I feel about the situation?

Is there anyone else involved?

What are they doing or saying?

Once you are aware of when, where, and what happened to you in your childhood, you can start to see where your acceptance and love originated, as well as who may have been involved in supporting those feelings.

More Questions for Acceptance and Love:

How good would I feel if I still felt accepted and loved?

How confident would I feel if I still felt pretty and strong?

How empowered would I feel if I still felt seen and heard?

How great would I feel if I still felt appreciated?

How credible or valued would I feel if I still felt respected?

As always, take some time to process what you are discovering and how it makes you feel.

Now that you recognize you once possessed empowerment, confidence, and value, you may choose to reclaim those abilities. No matter what your answers are, you can start to understand why you feel the way you do about yourself.

Follow-up Question:

How can I reclaim those positive feeling I once had, today?

Where Am I?

As you move through these exercises, you are becoming the master detective of your life. You are the only one who knows how you truly felt. You may need to evaluate every stage of your life, from childhood through teenage years, and even up to adulthood.

If these exercises bring up overwhelming emotions or anxiety for you, you may want to skip ahead and come back to this section when you are ready. You might also want to consider hiring a professional to help you work through your emotions. Remember, it's all about baby steps. There is no hurry.

Once we have formed a basis for how we see ourselves, it can affect our beliefs and behaviors for the rest of our lives if we choose to let it. These exercises can help you deal with past challenges that seem to repeat themselves, as well as the things you don't like about yourself. Here are a few examples of how I dealt with my insecurity and shame.

I have done a lot of work with my inner child throughout my life. I spent most of my twenties constantly asking myself the questions above. Throughout my life, I felt incredibly inadequate in my ability to read and write because of my dyslexia. I also carried shame for years because of the sexual abuse I experienced as a child. Below are a couple of examples of how I talked to my inner child.

Example I: Even in my twenties, I couldn't read, write, or spell very well. When I would go to an interview for a new job, I would morph into a nervous wreck. It would take all the courage I could muster just to walk in the door. Early on, when I would apply for a new position, I would take a piece of paper with me on which I had written down the names, numbers and correct spelling of the people and companies I had worked for. I would also write down words that I might need to use to answer questions on the application. I often struggled to read, and I definitely couldn't spell most of the information they required. Years later, I realized I had panic attacks every time I went to apply for a new job. When I felt my anxiety rising or panic emerging, I learned to ask myself the following questions:

1. **When was the first time I felt this way as a child?**

   Answer: In grade school. When the teacher asked me to read aloud, my anxiety became overwhelming. As I would stand up to read, I knew the other students would laugh at me.

2. **Do I believe I'm inadequate when it comes to my abilities to figure out whatever it is I need to understand?**

   Answer: NO! Even though I sometimes struggled to read or write, I knew I was smart enough to figure out almost anything. I have learned to ask a lot of questions, be creative, and remain flexible. These are now some of the positive survival skills that serve me well.

3. **Am I stupid?**

   Answer: NO, absolutely not! I can learn anything I set my mind to.

4. **Am I holding on to a past fear that doesn't serve me today?**

   Answer: Yes, I am. Then I tell myself the following truths: I need to let go of my past and do my best today. My best is good enough, and everything will all work out the way it should. Mannette, you are smart, and you are improving your reading and writing skills all the time. Hang in there; you can overcome this too.

Example II: As a young woman, I also had issues with guilt and shame. When I felt the need to share some of my story of abuse with someone new, these emotions would surface. I would stop and ask my inner child these questions:

1. **When is the first time I felt this overwhelming guilt and shame?**

    Answer: As a young girl while being victimized.

2. **Where am I?**

    Answer: With my abusive cousin in the barn.

3. **What is happening around me?**

    Answer: He is manipulating me into doing what he wants and telling me it is all my fault.

4. **How old am I?**

    Answer: I am nine years old.

5. **How do I feel about the situation?**

    Answer: I felt disgusting and dirty.

6. **Is it true that I am disgusting or dirty?**

    Answer: NO, of course not. I had no control over the situation. I was just a child.

7. **Does it matter to me now?**

    Answer: NO, the past is the past, and that isn't my life today.

8. **Am I carrying something from my past that doesn't apply to my current life?**

    Answer: Yes, and I can choose not to.

9. **Am I holding on to something that isn't true?**

   Answer: Yes, I'm not that little girl nor am I ashamed of my past. It's my choice to let go of my past and be the person I am today.

In both cases, within minutes, I felt more confident and remembered I'm not that little girl anymore.

The First of The Big 3: Acceptance

My wish for you is to embrace and accept the unique individual you are; your creator only made one of you. That means that there is no one in the world exactly like you — even if you have a twin! This is your opportunity to regain your confidence, strength, and inner peace. It is time to learn how to love, accept, and respect yourself unconditionally.

The following section is designed to help you learn to accept yourself just the way you are — no conditions or strings attached. No more, "I'll accept myself once I lose more weight, stop that behavior, or make an effort to change." It's time to accept that you are already a great person, even before you make positive changes. You deserve to be accepted, both by the people around you and yourself.

Stop and ask yourself:
Do I unconditionally accept who and what I am without judgment?

Perhaps you believe that you aren't worthy of acceptance until you have lost weight because your mother told you that as a child. Or, perhaps you simply overheard her saying that to herself in the mirror, and you picked it up as your own belief. Replace losing weight with nearly anything to make it personal to you, whether it is dressing a certain way, making enough money, dealing with addictions, the list goes on. Regardless of who told or showed you that you weren't deserving of acceptance, it isn't true. All of us have qualities or moments we aren't proud of. However, that doesn't make us inherently bad people. No one on this planet is perfect. Just because we aren't perfect doesn't mean we have to hold ourselves in contempt or criticism.

So how do we move past these feelings of not being good enough or needing to change ourselves before we are accepted? Let's start with negative self-talk and gossip. Over the years, I've found that these two things are the top hindrances to wholehearted acceptance.

Negative Self-Talk

There are two ways negative self-talk can be used: internal and external. I want to help you understand how your negative self-talk is impacting your quality of life, and help you become more aware of how often you think or say something critical about yourself or someone else.

INTERNAL: Internal self-talk is the full range of thoughts we have running through our minds throughout the day, both about ourselves and others, that can constantly trigger worry, guilt, hatred, criticism and fear. It's the part of your mind that is always on high alert and tends to overanalyze every situation and how you feel about yourself.

EXTERNAL: External self-talk is when someone verbally complains or criticizes themselves or others. You may know someone who always shares what they are thinking, even if it is better left unsaid. Words constantly explode out of their mouths, projecting how disappointing or awful they personally are or behave. (I'm fat, I'm lazy, etc.) They might even say critical or inappropriate things to others, especially people that are close to them.

Here are some examples of what internal and external self-talk could sound like:

I can't believe I did that.

I hate my hair, my body, my job, myself.

I shouldn't eat that, I'm too big / fat.

I never do anything right.

I'm a bad person—I'm going to hell for what I say and think.

I hate my actions when I don't have self-control.

I shouldn't act like that.

I hate my sister, partner, mother, or friends' behaviors.

I hate it when that person does that.

Do any of the above statements sound like something you might say to yourself or aloud?

It is entirely possible to learn how not to judge, blame, or reject yourself as you are right now! You have a **choice** to allow these thoughts and actions to rule you. It doesn't matter if it's an internal thought or an external expression; they both have the same negative effects on your mental state.

Like my mom always said, "If you can't say something nice, keep your mouth shut and don't say anything at all." She had a good point, and that goes for how you talk to yourself as well as others.

Negative Self-Talk Tracking Exercise

For the next five days, I want you to carry around a small notebook or make a note on your phone. Maybe you can call it, "Negative Self-Talk List." Every time you think or say something that is judgmental or critical toward yourself or someone else, I want you to write it down on your list. At night, take some time to read through the list and jot down the thoughts or phrases in your workbook along with the answers to the introspective questions below. Remember, you are discovering what's *behind* your behaviors and beliefs. Ask yourself the introspective questions below.

REFLECTIONS

- Do I really hate everything about myself?
- Do I really hate all my actions and behaviors?
- Do I really hate my mom, sister, or friends?
- Am I really a horrible person?

- Why would I say any of these things to myself or others—internally or externally?

- What insecurities might be driving these criticisms?

- Where is there lack in my life that leads me to be critical and envious of others?

- What things am I most critical of in myself and others? (behaviors, looks, possessions, etc.)

The goal is to become aware of how often, when, and why you use negative self-talk.

Gossip

Gossip can be defined loosely as talking about other people behind their backs, often involving information that has not been confirmed to be true. When we indulge in sharing or listening to gossip, it is just another way of being critical. Are you a person who enables gossip, either through talking about others or participating in conversations with others who are gossiping? Do you listen to someone else share their negative experiences or secrets, only to then share it with other people?

On the other hand, we have a choice to turn the essence of gossip into a positive trait. If you choose to inform others about the positive things you hear and learn, this can bring people together and make others feel safer talking to you. You can choose to share the wonderful and exciting things happening in your friends' lives, instead of divulging their negative personal information. How do you want to share information?

When have I delighted in knowing and divulging information that isn't mine to share?

When have I shared positive stories that might inspire others?

Gossip Exercise

Instead of writing down the ways you engage in gossip over the next five days, we're going to try something a bit different. I want you to make a note and share every time you see or hear something positive. It can be something someone shares with you, such as a compliment or encouragement. It could also be something that you notice throughout your day, like your server's beautiful smile or a stranger offering help to someone else. In either case, you can do something kind. You can tell the server they have a beautiful smile or acknowledge the stranger for their kindness.

You could also include a friend in the exercise where you text each other throughout the day supporting positive actions either of you sees or does. Once you begin to notice these things in everyday life, you can create a goal to share something positive with someone else each day.

At the end of the five days, take a look at all the good in your life that already exists. We all have good things in our lives; we just have to choose to see them!

Gossip and negative self-talk and are both rooted in criticism. Criticism single-handedly destroys any feelings of being accepted.

When someone criticizes you, it can feel as though you're being rejected. It immediately takes some people to the place of "I'm not enough." Good or bad, words have power. They shape what we believe and how we act. Critical words can often cause us to shrink and try to perform perfectly to earn our place back in the good graces of whoever criticized us. Words have the ability to attach and cling to us.

Close your eyes and imagine yourself covered in balloons from head-to-toe. Each balloon has a word on it to represent a negative thought or feeling. How hard would it be to get in a car, do yoga or go the restroom with all of these balloons attached to you 24/7?

What kind of balloons am I carrying around each day?

What kind of energy do these balloons project to the world around me?

What would it take for me to stop thinking negative thoughts or saying negative words?

What would it take for me to let these balloons float away?

Consider letting go or freeing yourself of your negative thoughts. It doesn't matter if you are just thinking negatively or talking negatively out loud; you are still projecting negativity. Remember, it's your choice, and you have the power to change your thoughts along with your life. Think of a positive thought as being strong and protective similar to a superhero suit, not cumbersome like a balloon. You are what you think. The more you think or say positive things, the more positive things you will receive.

How can I attract more positivity into my life?

How can I change my thoughts so that I am positively impacting myself and those around me?

Focus Exercise for Negative Self-Talk

For the next five days, make a conscious effort to replace your negative thoughts or expressions with positive ones (i.e., replacing "I am fat" with "I am perfect the way I am"). This may be challenging, and perhaps all you can do in the beginning is learn to not say negative things to yourself. Anything is a start! An easy change is to stop yourself mid-sentence when you realize what you say or think isn't in line with your positive changes. Make a note of how many times you were able to either stop or replace your negative expressions.

I also want you to make a note any time you had independent positive thoughts or expressions that didn't involve changing your negative ones.

If you have trouble changing a negative thought or expression, ask yourself the following questions that pertain to your situation. This is one way to break down your old thoughts and replace them with new ones. In the beginning, I often looked up antonyms in order to help me look through the lens of positivity.

REFLECTIONS

- What is the opposite thought of my negative self-talk (internal or external)?

- What good qualities can I see in others?

- Which friends, family, or co-workers pull me into negative expressions?

- Which friends, family, or co-workers pull me into positive expressions?

- How can I make positive changes with my self-talk?

No matter how long you've been engaging in negative self-talk and criticism, there is always an opportunity to turn it around. In fact, it is an essential part of rebuilding your self-worth after abuse. If you have struggled with this for years, reprogramming it could take some commitment and time on your part. You have a choice of whether you focus on criticism or acceptance. Whatever you turn your focus to is what you will create.

The Second of The Big 3: Unconditional Love

Similar to acceptance, it is often hard to believe that we are worthy of love without feeling like we have to earn it. You are worth being treated so much better than you may have been treated in the past. Furthermore, you should be the first one to treat yourself with compassion and kindness without any conditions.

What do you see when you look at yourself in the mirror?

Most of us only see imperfections and faults when we look at our reflection. Can you look directly into your eyes in the mirror and say, "I love you" without pausing or looking away?

I'm asking you to look at yourself and fully embrace the wonderful person looking back at you without dissecting every flaw you see. If you can only see a person who is fat, sad, lonely, or not pretty enough, it is time to work toward letting go of the beliefs that are holding you back.

Do you limit the love you share with others based on how skinny, smart, funny, pretty, or handsome they are? If so, that isn't unconditional love. If not, why would you limit the love you give to yourself based on the same conditions? Would you look at someone you love and openly criticize them as harshly as you criticize yourself? Do you really want to wait until you lose ten pounds or stop a habit you don't like so you can love yourself? Would you ever tell your friend that they couldn't try something new until they lost 10 pounds? The goal is to start loving yourself first from the inside, then accept who you are on the outside.

Life is a mirror that reflects how we truly see ourselves. The world has a way of showing you how you really feel inside — projecting both what you believe you are worth and what you believe you deserve.

People see you as you see yourself. If you see yourself through the lens of love, others will see the love in you. If you see yourself through the lens of self-hatred, others will see the same thing. The people around us often see our true selves even when we can't see it.

You can tell how you feel about yourself by the things you notice in others — either positive or negative. If you look closely, you will start to notice yourself in other people. However, this can manifest in two different ways. When you criticize someone for the way they look, you might be thinking internally that you are better than them (pride). Most survivors of abuse tend to see themselves as less-than or unworthy and criticize others because it makes them feel like they're not alone in their mess. Either way you look at it, we can still see what we need to work on.

REFLECTIONS

- What traits or behaviors do I notice in other people?
- How would someone else describe me and my personality?
- How do I see myself, others, and the world?

Creating Positive Self-Talk

Next, we are going to talk about *affirmations,* which means to affirm; the definition of *affirm* is to state or assert positively, as a fact, and maintain as true.

Contrary to what you might think, there is a lot more to affirmations than just saying a statement you want to create. In fact, it is a process that involves conscious thought that eventually evolves into a subconscious belief. Once you have a thought that has transformed into a belief — whether positive or negative — there is an unequivocal chance it will manifest in your life, according to Louise Hay.

Let's start with a thought or idea you want to create and walk through the process of creating an affirmation. It might be helpful to think about what you truly want and how it relates to what you believe before you begin this process.

1. **Be Clear:** The more detailed and clear you are about what you want, the easier it is to manifest what you desire. If you want a relationship, don't just say, "I want a new relationship." State what you want in your relationship or how you want it to look, sound, or feel. Try saying, "I have a healthy relationship full of laughter, passion, and kindness" or "I'm in the process of producing a great relationship with mutual happiness, unconditional love, and respect."

2. **Speak in the Present Tense:** Make sure your affirmations are stated as if you already have obtained your desired affirmation. If you want to manifest more security or wealth, you want to phrase your affirmation to say, "I have security and wealth in my life" or "I feel safe and secure with my financial situation of abundance that is evolving." Not, "I want to obtain more money next year" or "I hope my financials get better soon."

3. **Flip the Negative to Positive:** Your affirmations should always be a positive statement that includes what you want—not what you *don't want*. Instead of saying, "I don't want to be fat," flip it to say, "I am healthier by valuing my body enough to exercise and nourish it" or "I feel slimmer and healthier every day."

How and When to Do Affirmations

It's a great idea to do your affirmations in a mirror. Look yourself in the eyes, even if it is uncomfortable. I have found that the most powerful time of the day to do your affirmations is first thing in the morning. When we first wake up, our minds are clear and more open to new ideas. It's a good time to start in a neutral, calm place and attempt to maintain this demeanor the rest of the day.

Personally, I do this exercise in the morning as soon as I wake up—before I do anything else. Then, I try to hold onto my thoughts while getting ready for the day. The longer I hold on to these thoughts, the more connected I feel. Your goal is to do this exercise morning and night until you start really believing your affirmation and things start changing. If I have something I want to immediately change, I do my affirmations again a few times during the day. I use bathroom mirrors while I wash my hands, side mirrors while getting in and out of the car — anywhere with a mirror. I followed up by saying my affirmations as I wash my face at night.

In order to see continued growth, it's important to add new affirmations every three weeks to change it up and keep your mind engaged. Keep a list of what's important to you and what affirmations you want to manifest.

Examples of Affirmation Statements

This technique is based on affirming conscious positive statements daily. By reaffirming what you desire daily, your conscious mind becomes more congruent with your subconscious mind. In time, this technique can start to change your beliefs. The statements below are designed to help you start having a more positive perception of yourself. The purpose of this exercise is to make each statement your own, so you can fully own them. These affirmations will help you replace any old negative thoughts or preconceived ideas with new positive thoughts that will change your life.

Affirmation Examples:

I love you _____. (Fill in the blank with your name.)

I accept myself the way I am.

I give myself permission to be treated with respect.

I am learning to respect myself.

I am safe and secure.

I am learning to love myself.

I see all my magnificent qualities.

I'm learning to see the wonderful person I am, inside and out.

I am in the process of becoming more <u>trusting, honest, and happy.</u> <u>(Fill in your desires).</u>

I give myself permission to be loved.

I am accepting healthier people into my life.

I accept that I deserve to be loved.

It is safe for me to accept love.

I am healthy and happy.

I like my eyes, hair, smile, or sense of humor. (Fill in the things you like or love about yourself).

I am free to live my life and embrace all the things I desire.

I love myself no matter what has happened, and I always will.

I am a strong, courageous woman, and I will be okay.

I am learning to be compassionate to myself.

I give myself permission to have faith in myself and something more.

If you find it hard to think of things you love about yourself, the following questions might be helpful.

What have other people told me they like about me?

What did I love about myself as a child?

(Ask your family, children, friends, or partner what they love or like about you.)

What makes me special or unique?

Affirmation Mirror Exercise

Take your workbook and write down which affirmations you relate to or which ones you want to own for yourself from the above section.

1. Take out three index cards and write down the top three affirmations you desire and want to incorporate into your

life. You can use some from the section above or create new ones that promote love and acceptance for yourself. Tape your cards onto the mirror you will be using every morning and night.

2. Next, I want you to look at yourself carefully in the mirror. Look into your eyes and acknowledge the wonderful person looking back at you. Let go of any judgment or criticism and focus on the fact that you are a SURVIVOR. You are strong, and through everything that has happened, you are still standing. Remember, you are special, and there are tons of positive things you can discover about yourself.

3. Now stand up straight with your shoulders back and tell yourself you are proud of the person you've become. Now say your affirmations. As you walk through your home, around your office, or wherever you go, remember to hold on to your new confidence.

4. If you feel down, overwhelmed, insecure, or powerless at any point during your day, I want you to think back to when you left your home that morning and how you felt with your shoulders back and head held high. You can also go to any bathroom and give yourself a little pep talk by restating your affirmations. The goal is to bring your emotional state back to unconditional acceptance, self-love, and confidence.

5. In addition, I want you to say each of your affirmations out loud at least every morning and night. At first, it will feel a little strange, and maybe even inauthentic. Just keep saying them out loud and trust the process. Once you start to believe your current affirmations, you can change, alter,

or add new ones as you continue to heal. I did my affirmations for a minimum of three weeks before replacing them with new ones.

I know this may seem like a small thing, but these seemingly insignificant actions will help you feel empowered, whatever the day brings. Even if you don't feel like you are strong or powerful at the moment, you can learn to project that you are.

This is a classic example of how to fake it until you make it. You have the ability to trick your mind into believing what is true, even if you do not feel it. It may take quite a bit of time and training until you truly believe what you are saying, but I promise it will happen.

Note: You may want to make a few of copies of your index cards, so you have one set at home, one in your purse, one at your desk, and one in your car. Above all else, keep one copy near a mirror in your home you will be using for your exercise.

For the first couple of weeks, I want you to make a point to give yourself a hug, "Way to go, girl," or a thumbs up every time you do your affirmations. I can't stress enough how important it is that you support yourself emotionally while you progress through your healing process. Take care of yourself by being your own personal cheerleader and watch as change starts to happen right before your eyes.

If you experienced anxiety while doing this exercise, you might want to skip ahead to the anxiety section. You might find that you feel contempt, loathing, or even hostility for the person looking back at you in the mirror. If this is the case, go back to the first inner child exercise you flagged and find out when this feeling originated. Once you discover when and where it started, ask yourself:

Is this contempt, loathing or hostility I have for myself true, or is this someone else's belief?

How can I let these feelings go and see the wonderful person looking back at me?

Most of the time, we have to disprove the foundation of our beliefs in order to rebuild them. Continue with the inner child exercises to disprove your old belief system, then work toward replacing your belief with new positive ones like the statements above.

I remember the first time I did the mirror exercise. I stood there looking in the mirror, and all I could see were all my imperfections looking back at me: the bump on my nose, the fact that I was a broke, single mom without a good job. I wondered how anyone could love me, looking at myself in disgust and wondering if there was even a point for my existence. Even still, I forced myself to say things like, "I like my smile." However, my inner monologue would repeat that it was bullshit. To reinforce the positive belief, I would say it again. Every day, I would tell myself, "I like my smile. I have pretty hair. I am in the process of accepting myself with all the imperfections, as I learn to see my good qualities."

Over time, I became more comfortable and made a list of things I liked about myself. Eventually, I learned to say I loved — not just liked — myself. "I love you just the way you are, Mannette. I can see the wonderful woman you are becoming. Everyday, I'm improving my life for myself and my children. I am getting emotionally healthier all the time, and I'm learning to take better care of myself. I'm smart, loving, and deserve to be loved." In time, I learned to accept and love myself.

The Third of The Big 3: Self-Respect

Self-respect is confidence in one's self and a feeling that one is behaving with honor and dignity. I feel our self-respect is the basis of how we treat ourselves and how we allow others to treat us. Once we experience abuse, most of us lose our confidence and dignity making it hard to respect ourselves. Unfortunately, the repercussions of abuse can alter our character and how we perceive ourselves as a good or bad person. The key is to honor yourself for surviving and value the things you have accomplished; then others can honor and value you as well. Once you can accept and believe that you were not at fault for the abuse you experienced, then you can regain your pride and start the journey of learning to respect yourself again.

The questions below can apply to your past or present life.

What have I achieved or accomplished?

What qualities do I like about myself?

What have I done (or am I doing) that I'm proud of?

You must have at least one quality or achievement you are proud of. If you are struggling to think of something, ask a trusted friend or family member to help you answer the questions above. I've also included a few examples to help you see your value.

Example Statements:

I am an honest person.

I am a caring person.

I am a smart person.

I am a good mom.

I am a great friend.

I am a good daughter or sister.

I am an optimistic person.

I am a hard worker.

Write down which statements best fit your personality in your workbook so you can start focusing on your positive qualities. Also, write two of them down on an index cards and tape it to your mirror along with your other affirmation cards so you can include it into your daily routine, as we did with the Affirmation Mirror Exercise.

Examples of Self-Respect Statements:

I have ___ qualities that I love about myself.

I'm proud of my____. (Fill in the blank with your achievements)

I'm so grateful I have the ability to ____.

I respect all of my qualities that make me special, especially my ___.

This is a great time to start using the Hope and Healing for Survivors of Abuse audio. This audio contains background music with a voice overlay to help you reprogram your subconscious mind to become congruent with your new beliefs your conscious mind is learning to accept. Go to Mannettemorgan.com to get your audio.

Warning

It is important to distinguish that respect is never to be gained through intimidation or demands. In fact, intimidation breeds fear, and demands breed resentment. They are both abusive behaviors, and you'll need to make sure you're on the lookout for people who are masking abuse as respect. A good rule of thumb is that respect is about treating others the way you want to be treated while expecting the same in return.

There is often a fine line between confidence and self-absorbed. I want to teach you how to be confident and strong, not self-absorbed. David, my late husband, always said, "There is something to be said for understated confidence." I agree with him, wholeheartedly. If you find yourself becoming obsessed with the way you look, the things you do and the qualities you love to the point of only thinking about yourself, it might be time to reevaluate.

It's also important to maintain confidence without overcompensating for your insecurities. If someone is trying to make up for what they lack, they likely always tell you what you should do, or act as if they know everything. This behavior usually originates from deep insecurity and a need to be recognized.

Life is about balance; it's important to find your confidence without tipping the scale into narcissism or overcompensating for your insecurities.

When I was younger, I would constantly feel inadequate and get embarrassed. Then, I would try to overcompensate for my own insecurities. If someone asked me something I didn't know, I would tell them what I did know that was in line with whatever we were talking about. It took me years to learn how to say, "I don't know." or just be quiet and okay with not knowing.

 REFLECTIONS

- What do I focus on?
- Do I focus on negative or positive thoughts?
- Do I focus on negative or positive gossip?
- Do I focus on my challenges?
- Do I recognize and focus on my unique abilities or qualities?
- How can I improve my self-talk?
- Am I paying attention to what I put out into the world?
- What will it take for me to start accepting, loving, and respecting the person looking back at me in the mirror?

What Might Stop You?

When we choose to change or create something new for ourselves, there is almost always some sort of resistance. This resistance can look like anything from doubt to self-sabotage. When we understand these obstacles, it is easier to overcome them and let them go.

How Do I Feel?

If what you are affirming is in line with how you feel, that is what you will create. If not, you will ultimately get what you *feel* you are worthy of receiving. This conflict can create doubt and resistance within your affirmations. This is why I have altered the following "I am" statements. It is easier to accept the phrase "I am learning to love myself" than "I love myself wholeheartedly." Make sure your affirmation statements are believable so you can obtain what you desire.

You may feel unworthy of loving yourself as you say, "I deserve to love myself." Regardless of what feelings might be bubbling to the surface, you need to know you are deserving of love. As we worked through previously, these may still be learned feelings that have yet to be healed or even discredited.

Listening to Your Mind, Body and Emotions Exercise

When you do your affirmations, pay attention to how you feel. Your body knows your true feelings about every thought and idea you desire.

Find a quiet place to sit, relax, and close your eyes. Once you're comfortable, I want you to ask yourself the following questions about each of your affirmations that you're applying in your morning and evening routine.

Does my affirmation make me feel anxious or afraid?

Do I feel comfortable and at peace with my affirmation?

Does my affirmation feel true or untrue?

Do I feel good or bad when I say my affirmation?

Does my body feel lighter or heavier?

Does my affirmation make me feel uneasy or relieved?

These questions are a great way to discover which affirmations you may need to tweak so you can believe them.

TIP: Reword your affirmations into statements that you can believe and accept more easily. Here are some examples: I'm learning to accept ____; I am in the process of ____; I give myself permission to ____; I accept ____ into my life. The point is to believe every word of your affirmation.

You want a certain amount of passion in anything you affirm. It's actually a good idea to get excited about your new affirmations. Excitement is an emotion that can actually create momentum and attract your affirmations. Have you ever experienced the feeling when someone close to you has won or achieved something great? Their enthusiasm is contagious! You can attract that same feeling when you focus and get excited about your desired affirmation. If you approach your new affirmation with dread and apprehension, you are projecting uncertainty. If you approach your affirmation with passion and excitement, you will more likely attract your affirmation to you.

Self-Sabotage

As a survivor of abuse, you are going to need to be honest with yourself and make sure you aren't self-sabotaging your affirmations. We consciously want what we are affirming but can find ourselves subconsciously believing we are not worthy of receiving what we affirm.

There is an abundance of all kinds in this world, from love to wealth. If you were taught there isn't enough money, love is conditional, or only some people experience joy, you are living from a mindset of scarcity. This is the feeling of "Everyone gets what they want, but there isn't enough for me." Scarcity programming likely started when you were a child or experienced trauma. But remember: it's your choice to decide what you believe.

Here are two examples of how we might subconsciously sabotage ourselves from manifesting what we desire.

1. **Self-Love:** If you are desperately wanting to accept and love yourself but struggle to do so, you might be subconsciously replaying old beliefs from your childhood or your abuse. You may be holding on to beliefs you learned from your experiences and others. Those beliefs are 100% untrue. You have all the love you need within yourself; you just need to let yourself receive it wholeheartedly. Others may not

have accepted, loved, or valued you, but you have always been worthy of those things, and you are still worthy of them today.

2. **Weight Issues:** If you are trying to lose weight, but you don't feel safe and secure in your own body, you might subconsciously prevent yourself from losing weight. You might actually choose to hold on to excess weight, whether you realize it or not. We can use our excess weight as a way to protect ourselves from other abusers. You might be holding onto the weight in order to force others to prove that they love you in spite of your appearance. Once you learn how to perceive yourself as safe and secure, you'll find you don't actually need your armor of weight for protection. You can find comfort in who you are while transforming yourself into who you want to be going forward. You can start trusting yourself to set boundaries that keep you safe and protect you from future abusers, rather than using your weight.

Do you see yourself in either of these examples? Here are a few reflective questions for you to ponder as you move forward.

 REFLECTIONS

- Is there any downside to having my affirmation?

- If I have what I'm affirming, will it cause more change in my life than I'm ready for?

- If I choose to change, do I believe I will lose something or someone?

- If I have what I'm affirming, will it leave me vulnerable?

- If I have what I want, do I fear it will hurt someone else?

- Do I believe that if I have what I desire, someone else might not have what they need?

When I started doing my affirmations, I felt a little silly saying these statements to myself, and I wasn't exactly sure how to even say them. I started with a few statements that included things like, "I don't want another abusive relationship" or "I don't want to be so scared all the time." These statements weren't working for me because they focused on the negative I was looking to avoid, rather than the positive I was hoping to attain. So, I changed my statements to more positive ones such as, "I want better healthier relationships in my life" and "I want to feel safer in my life." But I still felt a little unsure and wonder if I deserved what I was asking for.

Later in my journey, someone taught me to change my affirmations to phrases that include "I am" statements. "I am capable of having a healthy relationship" or "I am safe and deserve to be loved." I still wasn't entirely comfortable with these statements, and I still didn't believe I deserved what I was asking for. Once I went back to my inner child exercises, I discovered where these feelings of unworthiness originated — my abuse. As I dug deeper, I started to find that it was all a lie, and my beliefs were based on what my abusers had instilled in me. I had been told that no one would believe me, and I was just an object that didn't matter. That was entirely false; those were their lies and beliefs, not mine. I began choosing to believe in myself and know that I was a good person.

So, I took my statements up another notch and said, "I give myself permission to have a healthy relationship full of kindness, compassion, and fun. I am in the process of learning how to be the strong, confident, empowered woman I was always meant to be." Something started to happen. I realized I could have healthy relationships, and the fear started to melt away. I started attracting healthy friends without drama, and my old friends began to disappear. I also attracted kind, compassionate, healthy men.

In time, a funny thing happened: I became that strong, confident, empowered woman I didn't even know I was capable of being. Once my affirmations were clearer and more defined, and I developed a positive outlook of my worthiness, things started changing. What I wanted started appearing in my life. What I didn't want started disappearing. I realized it was my choice to keep the good stuff and let go of what I truly didn't need or want.

My advice moving forward is to clean up your descriptions. Ask for what you want, and make sure your feelings, beliefs, and affirmations line up. Then things will happen just as they should.

We all know that a tree manifests from a seedling with the help of soil, water, and sun. Manifesting your affirmations is just like planting a seed and carefully tending to it so it can develop into a strong, healthy tree.

Perception

Everything I've talked about boils down to perception. You can choose to believe in yourself and your new abilities with confidence, or you can go on being a victim of your experiences —it's all up to you. There will always be challenges; however, it's how we perceive those challenges that sets us apart and gives us an opportunity to grow. You have a choice to face your past with dignity and compassion. You have the ability to face your challenges head-on and know in your heart that no matter what happens, you are a survivor.

Congratulations, you did it! You have worked through *the Big 3*. You are doing a great job! If you only learn one thing from this chapter, I want you to understand how important it is to unconditionally accept, love, and respect yourself because that is the foundation of your life.

This foundation is the root system of your tree. It determines how high you can grow and how you weather the seasons ahead. You want to create strong roots that expand deep into the earth. In the next chapter, I'm going to share with you how to strengthen your trunk through your behaviors, actions, and reactions. You will learn how your behaviors have shaped your life and how to change them.

One-Month Follow-Up Questions

After practicing your affirmation statements, I would like you to reflect on the questions below once a month for three months so you can evaluate how much better you feel about yourself.

How much more do I accept myself the way I am after doing my affirmation mirror exercises for a month?

1   2   3   4   5   6   7   8   9   10

How much more do I love myself after doing my affirmations for a month?

    1   2   3   4   5   6   7   8   9   10

How much more confident do I feel after doing my affirmations for a month?

    1   2   3   4   5   6   7   8   9   10

How much more empowered do I feel after doing my affirmations for a month?

    1   2   3   4   5   6   7   8   9   10

How much more self-respect do I have for myself after doing my affirmations for a month?

    1   2   3   4   5   6   7   8   9   10

CHAPTER 5

Embracing the New You

• •

I N MY MID-TWENTIES, AFTER I HAD been in therapy for some time, I finally chose to accept my part in creating a dysfunctional life. It was hard for me to take ownership of what I had created. I could have chosen to continue blaming my dad, cousin and ex-husband for my past abuse and my current situation, but that wasn't going to fix my life—no one else could fix it but me. I was a single mom struggling to make a living and constantly choosing relationships that were unhealthy. I didn't like it, but I knew in my heart it was time for me to take responsibility for my own actions.

I started by asking myself the following questions:

Why do I choose people that make my life harder?

Why do I have so much drama in my life?

What part do I play in these situations?

What can I do differently?

What can I do going forward?

What can I learn from each of these circumstances?

Once I chose to quit blaming others, learned to be honest with myself, and took responsibility for my choices and actions, it became easier to make healthier decisions for myself and my children. That is when my next level of healing really began.

Now that you have started nurturing your roots while letting them grow and expand, it's time to start taking care of your core (trunk). Your core includes your Behaviors, Actions, and Reactions (B.A.R.). In other words, your core is how you interact with yourself and the world.

As survivors, we have all learned how to cope with our abuse in order to survive. Some of us have acquired some destructive, unhealthy skills, while others acquired productive ones. You may not like everything you discover about yourself in this chapter, but honesty is the pathway to hope and change. This book isn't going to be much help if you choose to deny the truth of how you got to where you are today. You've likely heard people quote the second half of John 8:32, "the truth will set you free." I have definitely found that principle to be true in my life; being honest enough with myself to see the truth brought me a new found freedom.

What Kind of Life Have You Created?

The choices you have made have bred consequences that have shaped your life up until this point — whether those consequences are good or bad. You may not like this truth, but the fact remains: you are where you are today because of the choices and actions you made yesterday. Remember, you have the ability to make your life what you want it to be. Like I said before we are all products of our past because of the beliefs and behaviors we learned as children, during and after our experiences with abuse. However, once we understand those behaviors, we have a choice whether or not we are going to keep repeating them.

Note: Do not misunderstand me. I'm not saying you created or chose your first experiences with abuse. Our abusive experiences change how we feel and what we think about ourselves, which can then dictate our behaviors and actions going forward. In other words, abuse can cause us to change our characteristics and per-sonality, which in turn alters our behaviors.

Now that you've discovered a bit more about how you developed your personal beliefs let's start working on your behaviors, actions, and reactions (B.A.R) so you can make positive lasting changes. I realize you may have grown up believing that you exist in this world without any control of your circumstances. I disagree wholeheart-edly. Although I believe that each one of us has our own personal path or purpose, we each have the ability to choose how to proceed down our path and find our purpose. Our B.A.R create either a journey full of obstacles, disappointments, and pain or a journey full of healthy experiences, hope, and happiness.

REFLECTIONS

- What has my path looked like up until now?
- What have I created in my own life: obstacles or happiness?

Behaviors: Ways in which someone functions or conducts themselves, especially in regard to others.

Actions: The manner or method of doing something, typically to achieve an aim.

Reactions: The responses to treatment, situations, or stimulus.

Character: The mental and moral qualities that make up and distinguish an individual.

Survivor Skills: A developed aptitude or ability to continue to function or prosper despite obstacles or threat.

It's time to learn to be accountable for your choices. Every moment of every day comes with new decisions to be made, and every day, we have to take responsibility for the choices we make. In order to heal, we have to become aware of our *B.A.Rs (behaviors, actions, reactions).*

REFLECTIONS

- Do I like my behaviors and actions?
- How would people I love describe my behaviors?

- What do my behaviors say about me?

- What does my character say about me?

- What are my morals and values?

- Are my behaviors productive, or are they self-destructive?

I want to teach you how to start making better choices for yourself while molding your character into something extraordinary. The best place to start is by breaking down your old survivor skills and replacing them with new behaviors that serve you better.

Identify Your Survivor Skills

Be honest when reviewing the items below. Look at this as a learning exercise so you can discover more about yourself. This isn't about judging the things you've done that you're not proud of. If you have survived some kind of abuse, you have acquired some of these survivor skills.

I dealt with several of these survivor skills throughout my life from denial, rationalizing, blacking out, defensiveness, avoidance of people/situations, disconnection from my emotions, self-destructive behaviors, panic, perfectionism, self-mutilation, overcompensation, manipulation, lying, creating chaos and being a victim. I found ways to cope, and sometimes it wasn't very becoming, but my past behaviors don't have to define the person I am today. I had to learn to be honest with myself and discover which survivor skills I acquired after my abuse. Then one at a time, I change certain survivor skills and even let some go.

Below are what I will be referring to as survivor skills acquired to deal with abuse and the repercussions of it. Pay attention to which skills sound familiar to you.

Survivor Skills (also known as coping mechanisms)

- denial
- anger
- defensiveness
- blacking out/memory loss
- self-destructive behaviors
- addictions
- self-mutilation
- rationalizing or justifying the abuse
- perceptiveness/instinctive abilities
- humor
- flexibility/tolerance
- reasoning abilities
- persistence

Self-Protection

You may have learned the following in order to protect yourself:

- avoiding intimacy, people and situations
- unnecessary fight-or-flight response

- disassociation

- disconnecting emotionally

Control

You may acquire some of these behaviors in an attempt to control things or people as a result of feeling out of control:

- OCD (Obsessive-compulsive disorder)

- perfectionism

- hoarding

- unhealthy attachments to people, animals or things

- passive-aggressive behaviors

- abusive behaviors

- manipulation

- lying/cheating

- creating unnecessary chaos or drama

- strong religious/spiritual beliefs

You could have also acquired a panic or anxiety issue, maybe even PTSD (Post-Traumatic Stress Disorder) from the trauma you experienced.

Playing the Victim

Some survivors choose to be the martyr, taking the role of a victim throughout their lives. The following are some statements or thoughts you might see in this behavior:

- "I can't ____ because the world is against me."
- "No one understands how bad my life is."
- "My story is worse than yours."

Every survivor has been forced to try to cope with unhealthy circumstances. While some people find comfort in chaos, disorder, or stressful situations, because it feels normal to them as it is all they've ever known, others strive to control their environment. Some survivors use humor to ease their pain, while others hide from the world in seclusion because of their fear. We all find a survivor skill that works for us. Some of us even find comfort in self-destruction and dangerous situations, like those who cope by cutting themselves, chasing adrenaline, or becoming addicted to a substance.

Note: People that have never experienced abuse can find it hard to understand why some of us seek out these behaviors. They may struggle to find tolerance or compassion for us when we continue to exhibit these kinds of destructive behaviors, which can cause us to struggle with our own acceptance and self-respect. It's important for you to identify your survivor skills and realize that others may never understand.

Which of the survivor skills above have you used or experienced in your life? If you are struggling to recognize which ones apply to you, ask someone you trust which survivor skills you may have demonstrated. I have included more detail for some of these survival skills.

Addictions

Most addictions start out as behavioral habits we use for coping or suppressing our emotions. Addiction is a great way to numb ourselves or attempt to fill a void we constantly wrestle with. One of the most challenging things as a survivor is to face *what* we feel *when* we feel it. Addictions are a way for us mask or set aside our true feelings or emotions as we struggle to exist in our day-to-day life.

Even though we may first think of drugs and alcohol when we think of addiction, it can have many faces. It could be things that seem a bit more harmless, like food, shopping, exercise, or sex. Whatever it is that we are addicted to, it only comforts us for a short time until we feel the need to overindulge again.

Once a habit has turned the corner and become an addiction, there is still hope. Though it may be more challenging to change, there is always a way out. If you struggle with addiction, you might want to seek help from a specialist or an addiction program.

REFLECTIONS

- Do I have an addiction? If so, what?

- Is my addiction possibly something that I do in order to fill a void?

- Is my addiction an escape from my feelings?

- Does my addiction suppress my emotions?

- If you have an addiction, you are probably in need of something, and that something could be love, acceptance, or honest expression. The key to healing your addiction could be learning how to recognize what you are feeling in the moment so you can face each emotion head-on and work through them instead of masking them.

When you engage in your addictions, are you experiencing any of the following:

- Anger or frustration

- Sadness, loneliness or depression

- Fear, worry, anxiety

- Feeling overwhelmed by someone or something

Ask yourself the following questions:

- What am I feeling?

- What is my addiction giving me?

- Is it a temporary solution?

Most addictions give us some kind of comfort and security. We tend to self-medicate while hiding from fears, insecurities, shame, loneliness, worries, etc. Once you understand why you turn to your addiction, where your addiction began and what triggers it by revisiting the inner-child exercise in the last chapter, you can begin to address your addiction and replace these old behaviors with new, healthier ones.

I understand that alcoholism and drug addictions can have some genetic basis. However, it is my personal belief that we all have a certain amount of choice to submit to our genetic disposition or not. That doesn't mean we should put ourselves in situations that test our willpower. If you are a child of an alcoholic, social drinking could easily become a habit that turns into a full-blown addiction. No two people are the same. This is why it's important for you to evaluate your own life and family history so you can conclude what is healthy for you as an individual.

Self-Destructive Behaviors

Self-destruction can manifest in a number of different ways, not just cutting. We can choose to put ourselves in dangerous situations or turn to things we can't control in order to get an adrenaline rush or actually feel some type of emotion. Often, survivors who have experienced trauma with intensely emotional situations continue to seek out heightened emotions. On the other hand, we may subject ourselves to dangerous situations because we think we deserve to be punished or hurt. Some of us may continue to tap into our fight-or-flight response, which releases adrenaline and other chemicals throughout our bodies. These are some of the same chemicals we experienced during our abuse. All of these behaviors can cause our individual chemical balances to be disrupted and can create a continuous desire for adrenaline, dopamine, serotonin, and other endorphin chemicals. The ultimate goal is to stop or temper these behaviors, so we can stop disrupting our chemical balance and learn to live in a state of calm.

🍃 REFLECTIONS

- What kind of dangerous situations have I put myself in?
- How have I been self-destructive in the past?
- Am I an adrenaline junkie?
- Am I comfortable in stressful, chaotic situations?

After my divorce from my first husband, I became promiscuous. I told myself that I was in control of my body, and my body wasn't worth much anyway. Sometimes I made dangerous choices after numbing myself with alcohol like choosing to sleep with a guy that I felt I could control. The truth was, I wasn't controlling anything. I didn't value my body, and I wasn't getting the love and affection I desired. I just continued living a lie and served myself up for others to use. I told myself I was in control, and I was getting something in return. The real truth was I felt comfortable receiving negative attention, and I experienced heightened emotions while letting others use my body. Believe me, it wasn't easy to admit the truth to myself. The truth was I wasn't using anyone; they were using me.

Avoiding Intimacy

One survivor skill I see frequently is intimacy avoidance as a form of self-protection. This can be done in several different ways, ranging from emotional detachment to excessive food intake. Some survivors feel safer by remaining emotionally detached and avoiding getting close to other people—especially loved ones. It's important to distinguish that this doesn't always include physical intimacy, as was the case for me. Because some survivors don't value their bodies, they can become promiscuous through using their body as an object or tool.

As we've touched on previously, some survivors protect their body by using food not only to cope but also as protection. They feed their emotions and accumulate weight to produce a physical barrier between themselves and others. A survivor might produce obstacles, including weight or emotional detachment to test other's loyalty or determination to accept or love them. Obesity can be used to prevent intimacy and/or as a deterrent because the survivor doesn't believe they deserve to be accepted or loved.

Food can also be abused in the form of eating disorders such as anorexia or bulimia. These are extreme forms of control; if you have an eating disorder, you need to seek out professional help.

 REFLECTIONS

- When have I kept people I care about at a distance?
- When have I tested people's love for me in the past?
- Are sex and intimacy two completely different things to me?
- Have I ever had an eating disorder? If so, what kind?
- Can I accept that I deserve to love and be loved?

Attempting to Fill a Void

After experiencing abuse, we are left with a hole in our heart and lives. We may feel unacceptable and unlovable, so we may try to fill our void in other ways. We don't always fill those voids with the healthiest things; in fact, we can try to fill our voids with overconsumption. Just like addiction, overconsumption can appear in all forms including, hoarding, binge eating, shopping, sex, etc. Again, we use these items as a band-aid instead of dealing with our core issues, which are more than likely our old unresolved emotions, possibly grief.

A feeling of lack or unworthiness can lead to overcompensating for what we feel we are lacking. If you are seeking to feel more appreciated or respected, you may do more for others—even if they don't ask or want your help or you may feel a need to let people know how important you are or how much you know – seeking out acceptance, respect or appreciation.

REFLECTIONS

- When have I tried to fill a void?
- What do I attempt to fill my void with? (Alcohol, food, attention, sex, people, animals, etc.)
- How do I feel after I attempt to fill my void?
- When have I done more than others ask of me?
- When have I projected a know-it-all persona?

I have definitely attempted to fill my voids throughout the years using food, alcohol, people, shopping, and even sex. I always end up where I started, feeling like I've missed something. Not one thing I drank, ate, or bought filled the hole inside my heart. When I learned to face my emotions and grieve for what I had lost, that's when I quit hurting myself and began to feel somewhat at peace. I started to see myself as whole. As an adult, I finally took time to grieve for the little girl that lost her innocence and childhood. I grieved for the young woman that accepted abuse as something she deserved. As time passed, my grief passed, and my heart filled with new things like joy and love. In time, I healed, and I didn't need food, alcohol, people, sex, or stuff to feel complete anymore.

Intense or Void Emotions

Even from a young age, we can learn how to shut emotions down after abuse in order to cope. On the flip side, some of us can feel like we are drowning in our emotions. We can experience one or both of these behaviors at different times throughout our lives.

Are you a survivor that expresses your emotions instantaneously and intensely? (defensive, angry, or over-reactive) Are you the type of person who finds yourself almost void of any emotions? (cold and distant) Chaos and drama can be two of the most destructive things that we create or gravitate towards in order to cope. I know this may sound strange, but some survivors grow up with families full of unhealthy, chaotic behaviors that become habitual. When things are calm, we can feel uncomfortable and don't know how to act.

🍃 REFLECTIONS

- When I get angry, do I find myself somewhat out of control?

- When I get stressed, does it turn into anxiety or panic?

- Do I feel comfortable with drama or even create drama in my relationships?

- Have I ever created chaos when things are going along smoothly?

- Have people told me that I can be over the top when expressing myself?

- Have I ever felt void of emotions?

- Have I found myself feeling numb or disconnected from the world or others?

- Have I suppressed my emotions? When? Why?

- Have I ever been told I don't express any emotions or feelings?

It's always best to express your emotions as they arise, just as long as you can maintain some kind of self-control. It can cause emotional and physical damage if you continue to suppress your emotion; it is important to release your emotions in a safe, healthy way.

I remember when it was much easier to be checked out, especially when I was being abused. I would separate from my physical body (out-of-body experience) and watch from a distance to escape my sexual abuse. Once I was grown, I continued to disengage when situations were uncomfortable, scary, painful, or emotional.

That disconnection made it difficult for me to experience emotions when they were happening. It had become much easier to shut down and escape than deal with my present situation. I was missing out on all parts of my life - the challenging along with the good.

Manipulation

Some survivors repeat what they learn and become manipulative, passive-aggressive, and abusive. Your abuser learned their behaviors from somewhere and chose to repeat them, but you don't have to. All of us have behaved in some way we aren't proud of at one point or another. We are all human, bad things can happen to good people, and good people can do bad things. No matter what our past looks like, we all have the opportunity to become better people; it just requires some effort of our part.

If you have a tendency to be manipulative or passive-aggressive, take this as your warning before it goes too far. You have the choice to face your destructive behaviors or ignore them. If you've hurt people along the way, take some time to apologize. You don't need to carry guilt or shame for any of your behaviors in the past; simply make amends and move forward. If any of this sounds familiar, it might be time to seek professional help in order to get a hold on your abusive behaviors.

🍃 REFLECTIONS

- Have I found myself using manipulation to get what I needed or wanted?

- Have I been passive-aggressive in my relationships?

- Have I ever been abusive to someone else?

- Have I apologized or made amends with people I've hurt with my inappropriate behaviors?

Secrets and Lying

Lying and hiding the truth are just more survivor skills we pick up along the way. We learn how to lie and live without being totally honest with ourselves and others. Lying can sometimes be a necessary skill when we are surviving abuse, but it's also one of the most difficult skills to let go of, apart from addiction. When you live through abuse, you learn to be a really good keeper of secrets. It takes courage to learn how to share your truth.

Some of us live in fear of others discovering our secret because of the shame we carry. Others of us hide our secret because of the lies we have been told by our abuser. Some of us hide our truth because the humiliation is just too much to bear. You may have tried to tell someone, and no one believed you or told you it didn't matter. Whatever the reason, it taught you to lie and hide more than just your abuse. It could have taught you to lie or hide your emotions, challenges, who you are, what you need, what you want, etc. You have a choice to start being more honest with yourself and others, and it starts now.

🍃 REFLECTIONS

- Have I learned to hide who I am and what I want?

- Have I learned to only tell partial truths?

- Have I learned to lie in order to protect myself?

- Have I lied to avoid the circumstances of my actions?

- Have I lied even when I didn't really need to?

- Have I lied to hide my challenges?

- Does my lying serve me well now, or does it cause me drama?

The Victim

A large part of healing is learning to be accountable and responsible for your own stuff. This includes your challenges, issues, and self-worth. If you continue to blame your circumstances and behavior on people or the world around you, you will never fully heal. Though you were a victim of abuse, that does not mean you will always be the victim. It's time to move forward—step out from your old identity as a victim, and into your new identity as a survivor. Stop trying to hold others responsible for your past or present life.

Do any of the following sound like you?

- *I am this way because ____ happened to me.*

- *My life is terrible because I was abused.*

- *Everything bad always happens to me.*

- *I'm ____ because my mom/dad/guardian were dysfunctional.*

- *I'm ____ because my parents got divorced.*

- *I'm ____ because my parents didn't protect me from my abuser.*

- *I'm ____ because of ____.*

If you identify with any of those statements, I have some harsh truth for you: you need to own your own shit. Quit labeling yourself as the victim and let go of your past. Start owning your life and take responsibility for where you are today and how you got here. The longer you blame others for your situation or life, the longer it takes to heal and move forward. You can walk around with a banner over your head that says *victim*, or you can choose to wear the banner that says: *I am woman. Hear me, see me; I am a survivor.*

You can make your story into whatever you want it to be; you can choose whether you want to play the victim or the hero. It's important to realize the past is the past, and you are living in the now. No matter what happened to you, it's over. Now your job is to pick up the pieces and make a life for yourself moving forward. I'm not discounting what happened to you or anyone else, but each one of us has to move on with life after abuse. It's up to you to make your life better or you can stay in the pain of your past.

REFLECTIONS

- Have I blamed others for my challenges or issues?

- Have I tried to force others to take responsibility for my past or present situations?

- Have I blamed others for my misfortune, pain, or unhappiness?

- Do I feel my situation is always someone else's fault?
- What banner am I holding over my head? Victim or survivor?
- What character do I want to play in my story: victim or hero?

Understand Your Survivor Skills

It's time to face the fact that some of your survivor skills aren't helping you anymore. You might want to give yourself permission to accept that you are imperfect, and we have all acquired survivor skills we wish we hadn't! The ultimate goal is to let go of your destructive skills, so you have room to replace them with new healthy behaviors.

I would like you also to acknowledge that some of these survivor skills/behaviors have actually been a tremendous help to you. They've helped you cope, function, survive, and even fulfill certain needs. You may have also acquired some beneficial skills along the way, such as the ability to be tolerant or remain calm in stressful circumstances. You may have some hidden gems you could take advantage of in your career or day-to-day life. You will probably also have some survivor skills that just need to be tempered or toned down. We will evaluate your positive and negative skills so you can decide which ones benefit you and which ones are destructive.

For example: I tend to be a perfectionist bordering on OCD, which has served me well professionally. I'm organized and exceptional at noticing details. This was a great quality most of the time until it got to the point where I was so consumed with organizing and cleaning that I didn't enjoy my children or my life. On the contrary, I have struggled with being so tolerant I have rationalized abusive behaviors, which caused me to stay in an abusive relationship.

Positive and Negative Skills Exercise

Take out your *Finding Your Voice* workbook and make two different sections: one for positive (beneficial) skills and one for negative (destructive) skills. Then go back to the Identify Your Survivor Skills exercise and list all of the skills and behaviors you have discovered up to this point. Some of them may have positive and negative qualities and fit into both sections like my perfectionism and tolerance.

Which of my skills are beneficial?

Which of my skills are destructive?

Beneficial Skills Exercise

Go through your skills from above that are in the positive/beneficial column. *Finding Your Voice* workbook and write down your responses to the following questions.

Which skills might benefit me and my current life?

Which skills might benefit me in my career?

Do I have any skills that could benefit me in my relationships?

Next, go through the skills from above that fall under both positive and negative columns and answer the following questions:

Which skills might be positive and destructive at the same time, depending on how I use them?

Which beneficial skills do I need to adjust?

Which skills can I temper so they don't become a negative skill?

Destructive Skills Exercise

Let's address those skills causing you more harm than good, your destructive skills. Take your *Finding Your Voice* workbook and ask yourself the following questions for each negative skill.

Which of my skills caused me issues, drama, or pain?

Which of my skills have cost me relationships?

Which of my skills do I feel I can't live without?

Which of my skills can I live without?

Which of my skills do I want to eliminate?

I suggest you start with the survivor skills you are most motivated to eliminate (and feel you can live without). Avoid starting with the ones you feel you can't live without. Save those for once you have conquered some of the others and are feeling more confident.

It is important to take this one step (and one skill) at a time. Changing these skills may require time and work reprogramming your thoughts and behaviors so you can make lasting changes. You can use the exercises below to investigate when, where, and why you incorporated these skills or behaviors into your life. When you understand why you acquired a skill in the first place, it can sometimes make it easier to let go of it now. The *Finding Your Voice* Healing Audio on my website, will help with the reprogramming process at Mannettemorgan.com

When, Where and Why Your Survivor Skills Originated

Moving forward, we are going to use the same format from the inner child exercises in the previous chapters. This exercise can work for any situation or time in your life. Document your answers and how you feel.

Step One:

1. You can sit up straight or lie down, whichever feels best for you. Close your eyes and slowly take three deep breaths while you relax your mind and body.

2. Imagine a white, almost clear protective bubble surrounding you.

3. Once you feel safe and protected, relax every part of your body as you breathe deeply, starting with your feet and legs. Move slowly up through your hips and stomach, your chest and arms, and finally, your neck and head.

Step Two:

Now you are ready. Start by asking yourself the questions below. Whenever it seems right to you, pause and give yourself space to answer the questions.

Questions for Reconnection:

1. When was the first time I experienced my destructive skill/behavior?

2. Where was I?

3. What was happening around me?

4. How old was I?

5. How did I feel about the situation?

6. Is there anyone else involved?

7. What are they doing or saying?

🍃 REFLECTIONS

- Why did I choose to participate in this survivor skill/behavior?

- What did (or do) I get from this survivor skill/behavior?

- Does this survivor skill/behavior comfort me or fill a void in some way? How?

- Does this survivor skill/behavior protect me or help me cope with my emotions? How?

- Does this survivor skill/behavior give me some kind of excitement? How?

- Does my survivor skill/behavior interfere with any of my relationships? How?

- Am I choosing to continue with a survivor skill/behavior from my past that doesn't serve me in the same way now?

- How do I feel before I proceed with my survivor skill/behavior?

- How do I feel after I partake in my survivor skill/behavior?

- Is this survivor skill/behavior something I still need now? Why?

- Do I want to choose to keep this survivor skill/behavior? Why?

- What will it take for me to choose to let go of this survivor skill/behavior if it isn't helping me today?

I reached the point of being completely honest with myself when I was 25 years old. I was horrified. I didn't like facing my flaws, especially since I was a perfectionist. Wouldn't you know, perfectionism just so happens to be one of my destructive and beneficial survivor skills. I eventually had to learn how to temper my perfectionism. I could hardly believe how many survivor skills I had acquired throughout the years. At first, I felt disappointed and overwhelmed with all my unwanted and unflattering survivor skills. Then, one day, I realized my abuse had made me a survivor. The survivor in me knew that if I could survive childhood sexual abuse and the mental and emotional abuse, changing my survival skills wasn't anything compared to surviving my life up to this point.

urse, I was scared and constantly worried about how I was going to make so many changes in my life while working and being a single mom. I knew in my heart I had to let go of some of my destructive skills. For example, justifying bad behavior in people I have relationships with, seeking men and alcohol to fill my void and procrastinating to the point that I would cause myself stress, anxiety, and chaos. I just took on each survivor skill one at a time.

I remember the day when my aunt gave me the following quote. It was a gift in my darkest time of healing. "When you come to the edge of all the light you have and must take a step into the darkness of the unknown, believe that one of two things will happen. Either there will be something solid for you to stand on or you will be taught how to fly." Patrick Overton. At the time, it felt as if this quote saved my life and gave me hope. It helped me see that there is always light at the end of the tunnel, that there is always another day to do something different, and eventually, I could learn how to fly.

I believe it's a good idea to find your own inspirational quote, song, line from a movie or place that you can always go or recall during your most challenging healing moments. Find something that is meaningful to you and keeps you motivated to keep moving forward.

If you are feeling a little overwhelmed, it's okay. Take your time. Don't give up! You can do this. People all over the world make changes every day, and you can too. Just keep putting one foot in front of the other and hold on to the idea of getting better as you heal.

Emotional Uprising

Now that you're more aware of how you feel let's deal with some of your emotions. Yes, we need to look at those scary, erratic feelings most survivors hate facing. I realize, it's easier to avoid our emotions, but without experiencing emotions, we can't truly experience life. We are going to work through what I call the Emotional Uprising.

I believe that if you suppress your emotions they will eventually find a way to ooze out, similarly to an infected wound that has been neglected. They can cause you emotional distress, physical ailments and/or even disease. According to Louise Hay and Mona Lisa Schulz MD, Ph.D. in their book *All is Well,* emotions are related to physical ailments.[1] I wholeheartedly agree with them and believe our emotions can alter our cellular makeup and chemical production.

I have personally had unexplainable physical issues at different times in my life. As I researched each ailment, they have been connected to different emotional experiences throughout my life. Each ailment seemed to emerge after I had experienced a traumatic incident. Once I emotionally dealt with my experience, my health improved. No emotions are worth destroying your physical or emotional well-being.

It's critical that you give yourself the gift of feeling and learn how to express your emotions when they arise. The key is to express

---

1. *All is Well: Heal Your Body with Medicine, Affirmations, and Intuition* by Louise Hay and Mona Lisa Schulz M.D. Ph.D.

them appropriately, honestly, and in a safe environment. We are all human, and being human is experiencing life with feeling.

Babies have a lot to teach us. Babies express their feelings freely. It's pretty easy to recognize if a baby is happy or upset. They are always honest and live totally in the moment. They like what they like and don't like what they don't like. They also don't have emotions like guilt, shame, worry, etc. They are comfortable expressing their irritability as well as their laughter. We can learn from their honest simplicity and uninhibited behaviors.

From Happy to Sad and Everything in Between

Emotions are in constant motion, just like a pendulum that swings from side to side. There are varying degrees of emotions, from intense to indifferent, and each one represents how we perceive an experience.

As survivors, our emotions can be unclear and even messy. We can have trouble defining them as well as understanding which emotions apply to our experiences. Some of you may have been taught that certain emotions like sadness weren't acceptable, while other emotions like anger are used for multiple feelings. Your goal is to get comfortable and experience all your different emotions so you can live a well-rounded life full of expression.

I like to compare emotions to your vocabulary. Some people have extensive vocabulary skills, and others have a limited vocabulary to express themselves. The following section is to help you get familiar with the varying degrees of emotions in order to recognize which emotions you are comfortable using.

Varying Degrees of Emotions

I have listed some emotions below with varying degrees of intensity. (strong, moderate, and mild) Emotions are not always black and white; there are lots of gray areas along with variations. The purpose of this is for you to become aware of your emotions, along with their intensity levels. I want you to expand your emotional vocabulary.

Circle the emotions you seem to experience more frequently.

Draw a line through the emotions you hardly experience.

List of emotions:

STRONG	MODERATE	MILD
Overjoyed	Happy	Content
Awestruck	Confident	Accepting
Optimistic	Hopeful	Satisfied
Loving	Caring	Friendly
Confused	Frustrated	Uncertain
Isolated	Lonely	Excluded
Inferior	Inadequate	Inefficient
Depressed	Distressed	Disappointed
Degraded	Hurt	Unappreciated
Humiliated	Ashamed	Embarrassed
Horrified	Fearful	Hesitant
Outraged	Resentful	Impatient

Express Emotions

The list above can help you discern which emotions you are familiar with and which ones you are not. If you discover that you only experience a handful of emotions on a regular basis, these could be the result of suppressing your feelings in order to cope or survive. When you don't express how you feel, it can cause you to turn to an unhealthy survival skill. This is why it is important to acknowledge how you feel when you feel it with the appropriate emotion. You may have learned if you felt angry, it was safer to withdraw while avoiding confrontation than express your disagreement or frustration. On the other hand, if you tend to be an overly expressive person, that only uses certain emotions, (example anger or rage) you may want to learn how to express your emotions honestly with a certain amount of self-control. Besides, erratic outbursts lose their effectiveness when used on a continuous basis. So, it might be best to stop, breathe, and then express yourself in a calm, clear, and direct manner.

As I encourage you to express yourself, I'm not suggesting that you lash out at everyone who has hurt you. I simply suggest that you become aware of how you feel in each moment so you can express the appropriate emotion, with a certain amount of control, as you experience it.

The point of self-expression is to express your emotions honestly, both with yourself and others. If you don't like something or you don't want to do something, don't do it. If you feel hurt, express how you feel to yourself and others. If something triggers a feeling from your past, identify why, what and how you feel so you can deal with it.

Note: Before having any major confrontations with someone, refer to the communication portion of this book in chapter eight so you have tools to communicate respectively.

Unresolved Emotions

When you focus on your most trying experiences or challenges, it is easier to connect the dots and determine which emotions trigger certain behaviors, actions, and reactions. These same triggers can be the cause of your destructive survival skills. Once a pattern of familiar feelings has been created with a reaction, you have formed a habit.

Which of my emotions dominate my behavior, actions, and reactions?

As I referenced earlier, a person that experiences depression because of loneliness may choose to fill a void with food, feeding their emotions, which releases a certain amount of comfort, until their emotions need comforting again. This pattern repeats, and they never address the core issue, which is loneliness.

An acholic my try to avoid feeling negative emotions by drinking. They will drink alcohol to avoid, and escape emotions, unfortunately, this can result in depression, which is still a negative emotion. They repeat the process instead of dealing with the core, issue which is uncomfortable negative emotions.

This process can work with positive behaviors as well. Runners get a chemical high and begin to desire that feeling, so they run in order to release certain chemicals that reward the behavior of running. Running can become a habit that feeds their emotional and chemical needs.

 REFLECTIONS

- When I feel worried, stressed, or sad, do I turn to a survivor skill that involves overconsumption?

- When I feel frustrated or threatened, do I turn to a survivor skill that involves passive-aggressive or defensive behaviors?

- When I feel scared, angry, or worthless, do I turn to a survivor skill that involves self-destructive behaviors?

- When I feel lonely or disconnected, do I turn to a survivor skill that involves filling a void? (food, alcohol, seeking love, sex, companionship, etc.)

- When I feel anxious or stressed, do I panic or even run from the situation?

- When I feel depressed, do I find myself stuck or paralyzed?

- When I feel unworthy, do I find myself feeling like a victim again and again?

No one knows you like you do. The key is to discover how your emotions are related to your survivor skills. This awareness can make it easier to deal with your emotions, so you won't seek out certain survivor skills that aren't healthy for you. By understanding your triggers, it can be easier to change or let go of survivor skills that don't serve you. The more aware you are, the easier it is to change.

Understanding Your Emotions Exercise

Take out your *Finding Your Voice* workbook and document your answers to the following questions. I want you to become aware of which emotions trigger old survivor skills so you can start dealing with those emotions.

Which emotions do I feed, console, or suppress?

How do I feed, console, or suppress my emotions?

What actions do I seek out to satisfy my emotions?

Which of my challenging emotions from past experiences, affect my current life?

When and where did those emotions originate from? (You can refer back to the Inner-child exercise)

How is my current situation triggering my old emotion and behaviors from my past?

If we recognize and deal with our old emotions, it can help us let go of our old survivor skills, so we have room for new healthier behaviors. Then we can remain present and only deal with our current situations and the emotions that accompany them.

Change is How We Grow

This part of the process is difficult but not impossible. Change is a vital part of the healing process. Just like you, I had to learn how to let go of destructive survivor skills I had relied on for so long. The key to unlearning these survivor skills was being present so that I could see the situation for what it was, rather than reacting to an emotional trigger from my past.

How do you feel about change?

I realize change can be deeply scary for some of us, but ultimately, what we all want is to be happy. Your happiness may require a little or a lot of change. Change is constant, and happening every moment of every day. You can choose to either be an active participant or simply live your life reacting without any direction.

Once you recognize how your survivor skills started and why, you can make a conscious decision to release those skills that aren't serving you anymore. Only when we become aware of what we are doing can we do something about it and make the necessary changes. No one can force you to change. This one is all on you.

"Be who you want to be tomorrow, today."

Changing my old behaviors took a while, but I ultimately learned I needed to make different choices than I had before and stick with those new choices. Once I became more aware, I began to change each survivor skill/behavior one at a time.

When I was married to David, my second husband, I would sometimes have moments of emptiness and insecurity, even though I was in a supportive, loving relationship. I would try to fill that emptiness and insecurity with retail therapy. Buying something temporarily filled a void inside me. I was still working on my self-confidence and had trouble believing in my self-worth. Occasional retail therapy seemed to soothe my insecurities and fill my emptiness for a moment, but I always felt guilty afterward.

As a result, the guilt would weigh me down, and to deal with it, I would overcompensate by doing things above and beyond for David. Retail therapy and overcompensating were two old survivor skills I was still relying on. But over time, I learned to stop, think, and have a conversation with myself before using retail therapy.

My process was something like this:

Q: Why am I doing this (shopping)?

A: I feel insecure and empty.

Q: What is going on?

A: I'm trying to fill a void.

Q: How do I feel?

A: I feel as if I'm missing something.

Q: What can I do?

A: Consider if I really want this, whether it's something I can actually afford and whether I need it. If not, I can do something different maybe take a walk or go have a cup of coffee instead of buying something.

Through this process, I learned to only buy things I needed, loved, and could afford. I have tapered this survivor skill but, I still ask myself these same questions when I shop; or I do something else to get my mind off shopping.

When I stay present, think clearly and give myself a choice, I'm taking responsibility for my actions. Therefore, I didn't have to feel guilty or overcompensate for my actions. I made a different choice instead of reacting to a trigger or feeling with an old pattern. By making a different decision, I felt more confident and empowered, knowing that I made a better choice for me and my finances.

Changing Your Behaviors Will Change Your Life

No matter what you have been taught, you possess the capacity to change. Some say it takes three weeks to create a new habit; others say it takes six. I don't know how long it takes, but I passionately feel that once you believe you want something different for yourself, without question, judgment or doubt attached, you will be ready to change it. Once you believe in your new belief, then you can see it as something positive in your life. You don't have to wait three weeks or six weeks, because every day brings a new opportunity to choose who you want to be and how you are going to achieve it. Let's look at some simple ways you can start changing your perception.

Pain Versus Desire

Most people make changes either because they passionately desire something, or they are sick and tired of the pain they are experiencing. Passionate desire is a stronger motivator. Desire attracts positive emotions while avoiding pain is based on losing something. There is always more power in gaining than losing. Find something new you want for yourself to replace old survivor skill, so you are always working toward gaining something, avoid depriving yourself.

How do I feel when I'm excited about something new?

How do I feel when I obtain something I desire?

How do I feel when I deprive myself or lose something?

Removing Can't, Shouldn't and Should

Let's start by removing can't, shouldn't and should from our vocabulary. This one change can make a dramatic difference in your perception. By removing these three words, you will have less self-criticism, guilt, and regret in your day-to-day life. All three of these words will hold you back from achieving your new healthier life.

Start removing the following statements from your vocabulary:

I can't do that.

I shouldn't have done that.

I should do this.

Every time you use one of these statements, you are self-sabotaging, judging, limiting, or demanding something from yourself. I want you to step back and take ownership of your life while taking more responsibility for your words.

Become a Can-Do Person

Most of us have our own inner conflicts. There is a part of us that wants to heal and another part of us that feels safe existing in our wounded self. We all have two inner voices: one that tells us we *can* and one that tells us we *can't*. You are by far your biggest supporter and most challenging critic as you choose to heal. Choose new responses that invoke possibilities and choices like *I can or I could.*

Which voice do you most often listen to "Can" or "Can't"?

Here are examples of a supportive inner voice:

I can choose to do something different and healthier for myself.

I can change; it's just a different choice on my part.

I could do something different today.

I always have a choice, and I have the right to change my mind.

I can do whatever I choose to; it's all in my hands.

I can choose to make my life better for myself.

If you struggle with that inner critic always telling you what you can't do, go to the *Finding Your Voice Workbook* for more exercises. Start listening to the *can-do* part of yourself.

Now that you have a better perception let's become more aware of why, what, when and how you feel about your old survivor skills so you can choose to change them or maybe even let them go.

I C.A.N CHOOSE Exercise

Take your I C.A.N CHOOSE Cards from your *Finding Your Voice Workbook*. The I C.A.N CHOOSE steps are also listed here! You'll want to keep these steps with you at all times until you know them by heart and start making some positive behavioral changes. Put a card on your refrigerator, in your purse, in your car, etc.

I C.A.N CHOOSE Card:

I - Interrupt my normal behavior - Be present

C - Consider - Why am I doing this?

A - Assess my situation - What is going on?

N - Navigate my feelings - How do I feel?

CHOOSE - Choose something different - What can I change or do differently?

Repeat the I C.A.N CHOOSE process as necessary. It gets easier!

I̲nterrupt my normal behavior – *Be present*

Only when you interrupt your normal behavior and are present can you become aware of your thoughts and emotions. Being present can help you analyze the situation and make clear, sound decisions.

I realized I had to start living for today because honestly today is all I really have. I can't go back and change what happened or how I chose to cope with my abuse. I can only change what I do today. So, I choose to be present as I make conscious decisions and different choices than I did yesterday.

C̲onsider your actions – *Why am I doing this?*

Considering "why" allows you to discover what is going on. Why do I want or feel a need to do something that may be unhealthy or even destructive? Why do I act or react in a certain way? "Why" can help you discover how you got here.

A̲ssess your situation – *What's going on?*

Assess your current situation. What's going on? What is triggering this reaction? Does my current situation feel familiar or remind me of my past? How, when, and where? Does this situation trigger an emotion? Has this behavior become a habit or even an addiction?

N̲avigate your feelings – *How do I feel?*

Asking yourself these questions allows you to get in touch with your emotions and how connected you are to the behavior.

How do I feel about my situation or behavior? How am I feeling as my situation unfolds? Is this feeling triggering an old behavior? How do I feel after partaking in my old behavior? What am I getting from my old behavior? Am I replaying a behavior that isn't serving me in a healthy way? Confront and self-sooth your feelings and stop depending on your old survivor skill for comfort.

__CHOOSE__ **something different** – *What can I change or do differently?*

Become more aware of your choices and options. You have a choice to accept or reject your thoughts as well as behaviors, actions, and reactions. It's your right and privilege to make new choices for yourself and how you want to react to life experiences.

REFLECTIONS

- Are you consciously aware of the choices you make and how they affect your life each moment of each day?
- What kind of choices do you make for yourself?

Now that you have this awareness, you can do one of two things: you can choose to do something different or proceed with the same type of action, but this time in moderation.

First, choose to do something different.

You could consider replacing those old survivor skills with something different – maybe the opposite of what you have done before or a more positive new behavior. Remember the definition of insanity is doing the same thing over and over again while expecting a different result. Change is required to produce a different result. Work toward a different reaction/behavior:

What is the opposite of what I would normally do?

What new behavior would benefit me in a healthy way?

What new behavior would bring less drama or anxiety into my life?

What other choices do I have?

Keep searching until you find something that works for you.

You are now experiencing a period of learning and growth, which means you can change your mind as well as your behavior. Give yourself the opportunity to do things differently.

Second, proceed in moderation.

You can choose to proceed with your action or behavior in moderation. Remember, you are taking responsibility for your past, present, and future actions. This choice may require more self-control on your part. Take a deep breath and proceed with caution. Here are a couple of ideas that might help you proceed in a healthier way.

You may want to set some limits for yourself when it comes to substances. For example, if you overindulge with ice cream, you may want to remove it from your home and only treat yourself when you're out, or you could buy small prepackaged items. At home, you could designate a small bowl just for your ice cream.

You may even have to take more extreme precautions to control yourself. I've heard of people taping up ice cream cartons or putting a note on the lid, as the extra time allows them a moment before overindulging. You can use this technique for lots of consumable items.

When you choose to partake in a certain item, for goodness' sake, enjoy it and don't beat yourself up – really enjoy that experience and the moment wholeheartedly. If you have an uncontrollable substance abuse issue, please get professional help.

If you are a person that is trying to change an emotional behavior like overreacting to certain situations, you can learn the Belly Breathing technique in chapter seven or slowly count to ten with your eyes closed while breathing deeply, before you react or respond. You may need to consider physically removing yourself from certain situations; it can be beneficial to take a moment and process your thoughts before responding or reacting. If you find yourself needing time to process, you may want to let others around you know you are working on changing your behaviors. Then they can give you the space you need to work through your emotions and responses.

"Do your best, because your best is always enough."

Remember all you can do is your best because your best is always enough. Adjust, practice, and repeat each step as necessary. Eventually, you will find a sweet spot that fits for you. You can make better choices and start living a healthier life as you tame or omit your survival skills. Give yourself credit every time you produce a new positive behavior, action, or reaction. Consider how you might react to your child or best friend if they accomplished a great feat; you deserve the same.

When I started letting go of old behaviors while applying these changes, my life started improving. To this day, I always stop and ask myself questions. It's my way of checking in with myself to see what is best for me. I use this technique to live a healthier life. When I discovered I had a gluten intolerance, I used the **I C.A.N CHOOSE** process to change my diet.

I started by removing certain foods from my home, so I wouldn't have easy access. Next, I changed my thought process from "What can't I have any more?" to "What are my healthy choices going forward?" The biggest challenge was slowing down and thinking about what was best for me before I ate. After that, I started asking myself, "What does my body need more of?" "What would be good for me to put into my body?" I focused on what I needed and what would make me feel good instead of what I was missing or what I was losing. This part of the process was challenging in the beginning because I kept wanting to focus on what I couldn't have instead of what I could. Here is what I would ask myself when I wanted something that contained gluten or focused on what I didn't need:

Interrupt – *Pause*

First, I slowed down, became present, and more aware of my thoughts. I recognized I was about to act out an old pattern; then I asked myself the following questions:

Consider – *Why do I want to eat this sandwich?*

I love sandwiches. They are comfortable and convenient.

Assess – *What is going on?*

I want to eat something that I'm familiar with, and that is easy to prepare.

Navigate – *How do I feel?*

I feel like I could be deprived if I don't get a sandwich. If I choose to eat a sandwich, I will feel somewhat sick and have an allergic reaction.

CHOOSE – *Is that what I want?*

Not really. I'm tired of feeling sick and always having a stomach ache.

What can I change or do instead?

I could have salad and soup, it's comforting, and I love the crunch of salad. I could make a sandwich rolled up in a piece of lettuce or gluten-free bread with chips on the side; that could be satisfying too. I can choose something that will make me feel good and help my digestion system heal.

Next, I enjoyed what I had chosen while being grateful for the healthy food that nourished my body. Now that I've made this transition with my food, I have never felt healthier. I don't feel it is about control; I feel it is all about treating myself with kindness.

Do I occasionally think I want something that isn't good for my digestion system? Of course, but then I always go back through the **I C.A.N CHOOSE** process. What choice can I make that will keep me feeling healthy?

If I choose to have something with gluten, like pizza, I will have it in moderation with lots of salad. I accept my choice and always remember that this is just one choice for my day. My next choice is up to me and can be something healthier. It's always a process, and with each meal, I have another choice. As I get healthier and feel better, it gets easier to treat myself well as I stand by my new choices.

Now I can be proud of myself. I recognize my accomplishments, and when I make good choices for myself. I also recognize I am human and accept that I will make choices that don't always serve me in the best way. In other words, I take responsibility for whichever choice I make.

The **I C.A.N CHOOSE** process can change your life for the better. It is the best way I have found to make behavioral changes. It just takes time to adjust your thought process and reaction to everyday situations.

Obstacles for Changing Behaviors

Everyone experiences challenges as they change or let go of old behaviors. You may even hold yourself back if you are receiving some kind of familiarity or comfort from your old behavior - even if it isn't healthy.

*"Choose to let go of what doesn't serve you,
so you can make space for what does."*

REFLECTIONS

- Which survivor skills am I holding onto? Why?
- What am I getting from my old survivor skills?
- What could happen if I choose to let go of my survivor skills?

Doubt

Other people may echo your old programming or beliefs that tell you it is impossible for you to change. Don't listen to them. Protect and nurture your new behaviors as you give them time to develop. The goal is to believe in yourself and your abilities while removing any doubt that you deserve to be healthy.

REFLECTIONS

- What new healthier behaviors do I want more of?
- How is my new behavior better for me?
- Could I change? Yes, you could.
- Can I heal? Yes, you can.
- Do I deserve change? Yes, I do.
- Is it worth it? Yes, it is.

Analysis Paralysis

This type of obstacle stops you before you start. Do you question or overthink everything before you act? This can usually involve the *I can't* or the negative self-talk personality. If you don't give yourself a chance to change, you can't change. It's all about giving yourself permission to do something different than you have done before.

REFLECTIONS

- How am I overthinking this?
- How am I talking myself out of doing something before I start?
- Am I only seeing what I can't do or what can go wrong?
- What can I do to change my behavior?
- What are the possibilities if I make a change?

Pain of Change

It's human nature to avoid pain, and some of you may associate change with pain. Change can be quite uncomfortable; don't let the familiarity or comfort of old survivor skills detour you from obtaining your new desired behaviors.

REFLECTIONS

- How painful are my survivor skills?
- What will it take for me to accept that change is a process?

Note: Think about this. It can take more effort, energy, and money to keep up most old survivor skills. For example, it takes more effort and money to eat, drink or smoke more than not. It actually takes more effort to lie and manipulate than to be truthful and honest.

Unhealthy Normal

If you were exposed to chaos, dysfunction, or abuse since childhood, you may find a sense of normalcy in painful or stressful situations. What *feels* normal to you may not be the healthy normal you are seeking going forward.

 REFLECTIONS

- When have I created drama, unease, chaos, and friction in my own life?

- Have I thrived in stressful situations?

- Do my friends or family have lots of drama?

- Why am I always involved in other people's drama or problems?

- How often am I waiting for something to go wrong?

- How often am I comfortable with challenging partners and friends?

- How often am I comfortable with people who are calm and show me support, or do I find these kinds of people boring?

In high school, I was unaware of how I would create my own chaos through procrastination. I would delay paying speeding tickets, renewing car tags, and completing school projects, in order to create impossible deadlines and stress for myself. I would let my room become a total disaster week-to-week knowing that it had to be clean or my mother wouldn't let me go out on Friday night.

I picked relationships that were chaotic and full of drama for years. Years later, I realized my normal, comfort zone was chaos, stress, and anxiety even though it wasn't healthy for me. Once I became aware of what I considered to be normal, I changed my perception and learned to accept a healthier normal with structure, calmness, and support.

Mistakes

Mistakes are the stepping stones of change. You will go back and forth with new and old behaviors. You will find yourself reverting to what you know from time to time until you make lasting, healthier changes. You have an opportunity to learn from your challenges, misfortunes, and mistakes: these things can help you grow into a beautiful, resilient person.

> *"We all fall down, and we all have a choice
> to get up and try something different."*

Remember change is a process, especially as you omit or replace old survivor skills. When you face challenges or fall down as you make changes, I want you to ask yourself the following questions:

🍃 REFLECTIONS

- How many mistakes have I made in my life?

- When I'm learning something new, do I get it right the first time or does it take practice?

- Don't forget, your best is always enough.

Start Setting Boundaries

As you work on letting go of destructive behaviors, you have to limit your relationships with people who have negative or destructive behaviors. You always have a choice – even if it doesn't feel like you do. It's your choice to set limits, protect yourself and make healthy choices. It can seem difficult to set healthy boundaries with people you love and who you are close to, but it is a necessary part of healing. I further discuss boundaries in chapter eight.

🍃 REFLECTIONS

- When do I let others control or influence my actions?

- When do I have limits on what I will or will not do?

- How often do I say yes to other people when I would rather say no?

- How often do I make my own decisions, or do I let others make them for me?

Be Forewarned: Your Changes Can Impact Your Relationships

As you make behavioral changes, you will lose patience and get frustrated with yourself and others. As you grow, you might find yourself becoming more independent, opinionated, and empowered. This is normal as you make changes. Some of you may still have relationships that are emotionally co-dependent, manipulative, or even abusive in some form. Keep in mind, you have acted a certain way for years and tolerated certain behaviors that you're no longer tolerating; as you change, it causes a ripple effect in your relationships. Others can fear change just like you. You are learning and growing, but that doesn't mean others around you will do the same. Not everyone is going to accept your new behaviors with the same enthusiasm or determination you may have.

Surrender your need to be right, to prove your new behaviors or beliefs to others. Learn to let go of any need to justify, defend yourself or dominate others with your new beliefs or behaviors. This is a defining moment in your life, not theirs.

Some people will try to convince you they know what is best for you, even saying you don't need to change. These kinds of comments come from people that fear the unknown or are afraid of what will happen if you do change. Remain diligent in your new behaviors and be tolerant of others that don't see the same value you do.

 REFLECTIONS

- Are people close to me trying to tell me what to do or deter me from changing?

- Do these people have healthy physical, mental, or emotional lives?

- Do these people have healthy relationships?

- Are these people happy and healthy?

- How can I start creating healthier boundaries?

Let those close to you know what you are working on improving, so they can be supportive. If they aren't, you might want to limit your time with them as you continue to heal.

Closing Summary for Chapter Five

Congratulations! You did it! You have worked through the second resource of the healing process: *Embracing the New You*. This is probably the hardest part of the healing process, as change is always challenging. This chapter has been all about the survivor skills that helped you manage your life during and after abuse. By now, you probably understand which of your survivor skills have been detrimental in your life and which skills could benefit you going forward. With that understanding, you have become more aware of your behaviors, actions, and reactions (B.A.R). You have hopefully started embracing a *can-do* personality. Hopefully, you have started acknowledging and expressing your emotions as they occur. More than likely, you have learned how to approach and change some of your old behaviors by using **I C.A.N CHOOSE** process.

My goal with this chapter was to help you understand that change is possible, and you can make the changes you desire. You are doing great. Remember, it's all about baby steps. You just learned how to crawl. Soon you will be standing, and ultimately you can run.

You started your tree by planting your seedling, then you watered and nurtured your roots by implementing The Big 3 in order to form a strong foundation. Now you have started pruning those old behaviors that don't serve you or weigh you down, so you can make room for your new, healthy behaviors. You want to create a tree that is straight and balanced with a strong solid trunk. In the next chapter, you will learn how your tree's branches will ultimately reach toward the sky to manifest your desires.

 REFLECTIONS

- Why do I hold on to certain behaviors?
- What can I learn from my past experiences and old behaviors?
- Which of my old survivor skills am I going to change or replace?
- How have I started getting in touch with my emotions?
- Which of my survivor skills are brought on by an emotion? Which emotions?
- Is there someone trying to stop me from changing?
- Who are the people in my healthy support system?

Affirmations: Here are new affirmation statements you can add to your list as you work through changing or replacing your old survivor skills.

What is done is done. I did it to survive. Now I can choose to do something different and better for myself.

I forgive myself for what I have done and give myself permission to choose something different and healthier.

I am making better choices each moment of each day.

I'm improving my life by changing one behavior at a time.

I'm doing my best, and my best is enough.

I have a choice to make life better for myself and others I love.

I allow change into my life with grace.

I'm learning to change in order to have a healthier life.

I'm worthy of new, healthier behaviors.

I accept new, healthier behaviors into my life.

I give myself permission to let go of my old survivor skills while I'm learning to embrace my new healthier behaviors.

I'm learning how to recognize and embrace all my emotions.

I'm learning how to address my emotions as they happen.

One-Month Follow-Up Questions

After practicing the **I C.A.N CHOOSE** process and continuing with your affirmation statement, I would like you to reflect on the questions below once a month for the next three months so you can evaluate how many changes you've made.

How much easier is it for me to make changes in my behaviors after one month?

1   2   3   4   5   6   7   8   9   10

How much more infrequently do I repeat my old survivor skills after one month?

1   2   3   4   5   6   7   8   9   10

How quickly do I recognize which feelings trigger certain behaviors or actions after one month?

1   2   3   4   5   6   7   8   9   10

How much more in control or independent do I feel in my life after one month?

1   2   3   4   5   6   7   8   9   10

How much more empowered do I feel after making changes over the last month?

1   2   3   4   5   6   7   8   9   10

CHAPTER 6

Discover Who You Are

• •

I T'S STRANGE HOW one movie scene can teach us so much about
ourselves. I remember the first time I saw the movie *Runaway Bride*.
I particularly love the scene where Richard Gere's character asks Julia
Roberts' character, "What kind of eggs do you like?" Julia Roberts'
character, a woman who had broken several engagements to different
men, liked whatever kind of eggs they liked. Her character was a classic
example of someone who didn't know what she wanted, and more than
likely didn't value her own needs or desires. For whatever reason, her
character was compliant, indecisive, and passive in her relationships.

After I left my first husband, I saw myself in
her character. I too was passive, compliant, and
unsure of who I was or what I wanted. I had lived
most of my life never expressing my voice or
opinion. In other words, I didn't know what kind
of eggs I liked. Through years of therapy and lots
of self-work, I discovered what was important to
me. Now I can proudly say I like Eggs Benedict

with bacon, tomatoes, and avocado served over country-style potatoes, instead of English muffins, and with an arugula salad on the side, topped with lemon and a little bit of oil. I know what I like and don't like, including my eggs. I found my voice, and I know who I am without question.

By now, you are hopefully more comfortable nourishing your roots as you have learned to embrace *The Big 3* (acceptance, unconditional love, and self-respect) while applying your affirmations. Hopefully, you are strengthening your trunk by omitting and replacing old survivor skills with healthier behaviors. It's time to focus on expanding your branches and limbs, which in this case represents your needs and desires.

Most of us have spent our lives focusing on what we had to do in order to survive. We never had the luxury of taking time to concentrate on what we needed much less what we desired. As a survivor, we may have focused on what we didn't want; unfortunately, that is what we attracted and repeatedly got more of.

We will start with your identity; then we will focus on your needs. Ultimately, you will learn how to cultivate your desires. This chapter is dedicated to discovering who you are and the ability to manifest your desires.

Below are a few personality tests so you can discover more about your unique personality. Understanding yourself is necessary and beneficial to your healing process. You may even feel empowered as you become more self-aware.

- Meyers-Briggs Personality Assessment by Isabel Briggs Myers and Katharine Briggs; 16 Personalities is to help you identify your most prevalent personality traits. https://www.16personalities.com

- Determine your Enneagram personality type by Don Richard Riso & Russ Hudson. https://www.eclecticenergies.com/enneagram

- The 5 Love Languages by Gary Chapman can help you learn more about how you process love. http://www.5lovelanguages.com/profile/

Once you have your results, you can refer to your list if you find yourself searching for a new career, engaging in new relationships or experiencing challenges.

Knowing who you are can benefit you as you heal and grow. For example, I learned that I am the protagonist personality type (also known as an ENFJ in Meyers-Briggs' Personality Assessment) My strengths are being tolerant, reliable, charismatic, altruistic, and a natural leader. My weaknesses are being overly idealistic, too selfless, too sensitive, fluctuating self-esteem, and struggling to make tough decisions. Some of my strengths, like tolerance, have caused me challenges in my past relationships, I tolerated bad behavior in others for far too long. On the other hand, I put a lot of thought and analysis into making tough decisions, which has benefited me throughout the years.

Note: As you work through the healing process, your personality may change and evolve. You may want to revisit some tests months or even years later.

Once you embrace who you are, then you can pursue more of what you desire. Most individuals that have experienced abuse, trauma or neglect, especially as a child or adolescent, struggle to understand who they are and what they like or dislike.

 REFLECTIONS

- Who am I?
- What do I need?
- What do I like and dislike?
- What do I desire more of in my life?

Differences Between Needs and Desires

Desires and needs are a vital part of your life, even if you haven't acknowledged them before. Needs can give us stability and security while desires can give us comfort and hope.

Definitions

Need: A physiological or psychological requirement for the well-being of an organism.

Desire: To long or hope for; to express a wish for, crave, want.

Codependency: A psychological condition or a relationship in which a person manifesting low self-esteem and a strong desire for approval has an unhealthy attachment to another person and places the needs of that person before his or her own.

Let's break down the difference between our two basic needs. You have physical and emotional needs. Both are important to your survival even if you have ignored or neglected them up until now.

Physical Needs

Everyone has a certain amount of required physical daily needs just to exist like air, water, food, etc. It's also important to have shelter, clothing, a source of income, safety, etc. . .

 REFLECTION

- What do I physically need to exist and survive?

Emotional Needs

Emotional needs are just as important as your physical needs. Emotional needs can include happiness, confidence, and self-love. You might not have experienced some of these emotional needs if you grew up in a family that didn't support healthy emotions. You may have found yourself craving anything that resembled love. This could be one reason why you may have accepted abusive relationships in the past.

You could be someone that learned how to put everyone else's needs before your own, even to the point of becoming co-dependent. All you've known is how to give and give while neglecting your own personal needs, somehow believing you aren't worthy of your needs much less your desires. Listen, you are worthy of so much more.

🌿 REFLECTIONS

- Am I codependent?
- Have I displayed codependent traits in the past?
- When?
- With whom?

This is one behavior you may want to work toward changing, as it can impact your ability to fulfill your own needs and desires. If you always meet everyone else's needs and wants, there isn't much left for your own needs and wants. I'm not implying that you neglect your family or responsibilities, but it is necessary to take care of yourself as well as others. *Codependent No More* by Melody Beattie is a great book for anyone dealing with co-dependency.

Some of you may live in a state of depression, anxiety, or anger after experiencing your abuse. You may need to feel safe and secure, or you may need to find a certain amount of peace. All of these feelings could be due to a lack of receiving what you needed emotionally. Whatever your emotional needs are, I want you to become aware of them so you can make them a priority going forward. The next exercise will help you to identify some of your most important emotional needs.

Personal Emotional Needs Exercise

Using the list below, circle up to ten of the emotions you feel you need. Spend a few minutes and think of any other emotions you want to start experiencing more of in your life. You may even want to revisit the "Emotional Uprising" section in chapter 5.

admiration	authenticity	compassion	confidence
contentment	enthusiasm	fun	happiness
hope	inspiration	joy	laughter
optimism	satisfaction	security	self-acceptance
self-love	self-respect	self-tolerance	serenity

Emotional Needs Comparison Exercise

Using the *Finding Your Voice* workbook, write down and number at least ten emotional needs you feel are important to the relationship you have with yourself.

Once you have written down your emotional needs, move through your list with the following instructions: You can refer to the example below to further clarify the process before you start the exercise.

1. Ask yourself *what can I NOT live without?* Example: *I CANNOT live without self-love.* As you review the list, you may find some of your answers might be similar. **Example:** *I need to feel safe* can be similar to *I need to feel secure.* In

that case, choose the word that best describes what you emotionally need or combine the two, such as safe/secure.

2. Look over the example I have provided in order to better understand the exercise. Move through this exercise quickly. Don't think too much. Listen to your gut and be honest with yourself.

3. Once you have completed the exercise, list the emotional needs that have the most check marks in order of importance, the top three to five emotional needs are what you value within yourself. Respect, nurture, and make these personal needs a priority in your life as you continue your healing process.

Example from my Emotional Need Comparison Exercise

When I did this exercise, my list of emotional needs included serenity, self-respect, self-acceptance, joy, among others, but for this example, we'll use those four. My list looked something like this. The numbering is not necessarily in order of importance, but for the exercise I am asking you to complete, the numbers are needed for comparison purposes.

1. Serenity

2. Self-Respect

3. Self-Acceptance

4. Joy

I took the first Emotional Need in my list and began to compare it with the other 3. I asked myself the question;

What Can I NOT live without?

1. Serenity

2. Self-Respect

I chose Self-Respect, so Self-Respect got a checkmark. Then I continued comparing Serenity with Self-Acceptance, and then Joy. Asking myself the same comparison question, "What Can I NOT live without?" and put a checkmark next to the Emotional Need I couldn't live without.

Here is how to think about it graphically.

Emotional Needs Comparison

Comparison 1	Comparison 2	Comparison 3
Serenity	Self-Respect	Acceptance
1 and 2	2 and 3	3 and 4
1 and 3	2 and 4	
1 and 4		

At the end of the first comparison of Serenity to my other Emotional Needs, my list looked like this:

1. Serenity ✓

2. Self-Respect ✓

3. Self-Acceptance ✓

4. Joy

Next, I began with Self-Respect and compared it to the other 2 Emotional Needs, Self-Acceptance, and Joy. It may feel like you are doing the same thing, but our mind has a way of framing things differently when we give it a #1 or #2 type comparison.

This would be Comparison 2. Use the same list and add your check-marks to it.

At the end of comparing Self-Respect, my list looked like this:

1. Serenity ✓

2. Self-Respect ✓✓✓

3. Self-Acceptance ✓

4. Joy

Then I went to Comparison 3 (Self-Acceptance) and answered the same questions.

At the end, my list looked like this:

1. Serenity ✓

2. Self-Respect ✓✓✓

3. Self-Acceptance ✓✓

4. Joy

If this had been my full list, I would be finished. I'd then put them in order of importance to my life:

1. Self-Respect (3 checks)

2. Self-Acceptance (2 checks)

3. Serenity (1 check)

4. Joy (0 checks)

Based on my initial gut reactions, self-respect is my top priority, and something I need to actively seek for myself. Joy was at the bottom of my list of priorities, but that doesn't mean it is not important; it's still in my top 4. However, self-respect is vital to me, and self-acceptance along with serenity is important too.

Your needs may change and be re-ordered as you grow and become healthier. The ultimate goal is to understand what you need and don't need so that you can take better care of your physical and emotional self.

Desires

Desires are all about what you want, crave, and wish for in your life. If you could make a wish, what would you wish for? Do you even dare to wish for what you want or desire? Why not? I realize desires can be elusive. Some of you may have found yourselves chasing your desires, never obtaining what you wanted. Maybe some of you are like my daughter and know that you can truly have anything you desire.

Let's start with where you are now. Do you feel you can have anything, or do you struggle to accept that anything is possible? My hope is you become a person who knows anything is possible. Go through the questions below along with the desire list below; then I want you to do the inner child exercise following them both—document everything you discover about yourself and your desires.

What do I want more of in my life?

What is my ultimate wish for myself?

What makes me smile, no matter what?

What makes me feel alive?

When do I feel truly happy?

What am I doing when I'm having fun?

What activities am I drawn to?

What places am I drawn to?

What am I curious about?

What am I passionate about?

What do I think about or focus on at least once a week?

What do I make time for, no matter how busy I am?

What do I spend money on besides necessities?

What is truly important to me?

What fills my heart with joy and love?

What things do I do no matter how tired I am?

Ask a friend: What do I talk about?

Ask a friend: What do I get excited about?

Examples of Desires

You may want to clarify certain objectives, instead of wanting just a *relationship,* you may want a *healthy caring relationship* or instead of wanting a *career,* you may want a *new career with a certain expertise.*

adventure	home
animals	learning (cultures, technology, crafts, etc.)
art/photography	making something (jewelry, woodworking, etc.)
career (new or restructured)	
cooking	music
dancing	nature (hiking, camping, etc.)
exercising (running, yoga, swimming)	reading
financial security	relationships (friendships, partner, family, etc.)
freedom	
gardening	relaxing
health	social activities
helping others	sports
theater	volunteering
traveling	writing

Inner-Child Recall Exercise

Your inner child has some insight into your truest desires. The key is rediscovering what you always dreamed of becoming. Follow the steps from the inner child exercise you flagged in chapter four and document your answers.

1. Focus on the first time you pretended to be someone or something that interested you. Think about what you longed for as a child. **For example:** do you remember pretending to be a teacher, artist, veterinarian, explorer, singer, dancer, or the president? Maybe you longed for more love, laughter, adventure or joy.

    What did I dream of doing?

    What did I really enjoy doing as a child?

    Who did I pretend to be?

    What books and movies interested me?

    What did I desire more of in my life?

2. Go deeper, apply the questions below to each desire that surfaced.

    Physically, where am I?

    How old am I?

    How do I feel about what I'm doing?

    Is there anyone else involved?

    What are they doing or saying?

    Are they encouraging me?

Stop and listen to your inner child then write down your answers.

When I was a small girl, I dreamed of traveling the world, writing and talking to people. I would pretend I lived in a high-rise apartment in some city, and I would sit for hours scribbling on paper. Then I would give lectures about the things I "wrote" about. I wanted to teach and share what I knew with others.

As a young student, I realized I wasn't learning to read or write as easily as everyone else. Over the next couple of years, I became discouraged, and I gave up on my dream of writing and teaching. I thought I was too stupid – a belief that was reinforced by my first-grade teacher who told my mom and me that I was stupid, and she couldn't teach me, because I was hopeless. I thought to myself, *who would ever listen to me? I can't even read, much less write.*

Forty years later, I managed to find my way back to one of my desires. I discovered a passion for helping other women through workshops. Today, I'm writing books, inspiring and teaching other women how to heal after surviving abuse. The key for me was finding my way back to what I desired and having faith that I could do it.

Find a way to start integrating your desires and dreams into your life. If there is a will, there is always a way. Let's continue so you can discover which desires you want to pursue or reintegrate into your life.

Discovering Your Desires Comparison Exercise

Using your *Finding Your Voice* workbook, write down any desires that surfaced with the last three exercises. Include ten desires, or as many items as you can think of, then number them. Your goal is to discover the part of you that was lost, rejected, or never discovered. Proceed through your list with the instructions below.

1. Ask yourself the following question. ***Which of these do I desire most?*** Put a checkmark next to the desire that is most important to you. As you review the list, you may find some of your desires might be similar. If so, combine those into one item. Example: *I want more adventure* can be similar to *I want more excitement.* Combine them into one or put them together adventure/excitement.

2. Go through each desire separately following the desire comparison exercise method like you did on pages 160-162.

3. List the desires that have the most checkmarks in order of importance; the top five desires are what you want to seek more of in your life.

4. Now that you have a list, apply the top five desires to the following questions so you can see which desires are more obtainable for you in your current life.

 REFLECTIONS

- Have I ever experienced any of these desires in my life?
- Which ones and when?
- How can I see myself attaining these desires?
- How can I manifest my desire?
- What can I do to live a life with more of these desires?
- How can I incorporate my desires into a hobby or even my work?

Nurture and make these personal desires a priority in your life as you continue your healing process. Your desires may alter or change as you grow and become healthier. You may want to revisit this exercise over the next year as you heal.

Definition

Create: To bring into existence; to produce or bring about by a course of action or behavior.

Manifest: To make evident or certain by showing, displaying or proving.

Manifest Your Desires

Now that you know what you physically and emotional need as well as what you desire, it is time to start fulfilling those needs and desires. This might be a little hard to accept, but I feel each one of us has the ability to manifest what we need and desire. Like it or not, you are the creator of your life.

REFLECTIONS

- What have I manifested in my life up to this point?
- What do I want to manifest more of going forward?

"Every invention started with a thought!"

We are all creators of something. Every creation starts with a thought; that thought turns into an intention, that intention sparks your imagination and can evolve into a belief, that belief can lead to an action and that action can, in turn, create a desired outcome.

You can consciously choose to create your new desires through intention and action, or you can continue to create your past or present life through old beliefs and behaviors. Everyone has desires and dreams – some are small, while others are big. You already have everything you need to create your desires. You have the ability to think and do something different than you've done before.

> *"If you believe you can do something or if you believe you can't do something. Both are right; you manifest what you believe."*
> HENRY FORD

These are the steps to manifesting your desires. You have to stay completely present with your new intention, imagination, belief, and action. The more present and aware you are of each step, the easier it is to manifest. This section will explain the five steps I used to create my desires throughout my life. I have created an acronym: **SITT PATIENTLY**.

S - Set an intention for what I desire.

I - Imagine my desire in my life.

T - Translate my desire into a belief.

T - Take action to produce my desire.

PATIENTLY - Patiently wait for my desire.

Ultimately you will create a desire. Let's look at each one carefully.

Set an intention for what I desire

Intention is the first step to manifesting your desire. A desire starts with a thought, and that thought needs to become an intention with a certain amount of passion. Your intention can start the momentum that helps you obtain your desire.

Imagine my desire in my life

Next, imagine yourself living your new desire. Your imagination is another part of your thought process and a powerful tool. Your goal is to hear, see, and feel yourself having your desire within your imagination, which will ultimately reinforce your belief in your desire. Did you know your brain can't recognize the difference between your imagination and reality? It actually accepts both scenarios as real. Here are a few ways to use your imagination:

- Visualize every positive detail of you accomplishing your desire. Put yourself in your own mental movie. See yourself involved in conversations and actions as your experience plays out in your imagination.

- Imagine others congratulating you for accomplishing your desire.

- Experience how you feel when you have obtained your desire. Immerse yourself in positive feelings and emotions while experiencing your desire within your imagination.

It can be a good idea to practice using your imagination in a meditative or daydreaming state. Let your mind take you on an adventure while it creates positive details that fit into your ultimate desire. Use your imagination to transition your desire from your conscious to your subconscious mind.

What does your desire sound, look, and feel like to you?

How do you see your desire playing out in detail?

What are others saying about your desire once it has happened?

How does it feel to have your desire?

What are the rewards for having your desire?

Translate my desire into a belief

It is time to consider that we all live in a world of abundance and plenty. You can choose to have any of the following: happiness, love, joy, companionship, career, abundance, etc. The key is believing your desire is available and obtainable.

Note: Having what you need doesn't mean someone else has to do without. This is a myth. There is plenty of everything in the world. The secret is a distribution of goods and accepting whatever you desire with gratitude and grace. There is an endless supply of emotions, which include love, joy, happiness, etc. It is time to allow yourself to receive them.

You want to feel and believe you are worthy as well as deserving of what you desire, and let go of any fear or doubt. If you don't feel safe or secure having your desire, you will subconsciously reject it. Embrace your worthiness, knowing you deserve to have your desires or something better. The goal is to get your subconscious and conscious congruent, so they both believe in your desire, without question. You want to believe it to create it.

Note: If you struggle with feeling unsure or insecure in your desire, use the inner child recall exercise to see when and why this belief originated. You may be carrying a false belief that doesn't apply to your life now.

Once you believe in your desire, learn to have faith and hope that good things can and will happen in your life. The best way to sum this up is to believe your desire is available and obtainable, believe you deserve your desire, believe in something bigger and most of all believe in yourself.

Can you believe there is abundance in the world?

What will it take for to you believe you can achieve your desire?

What will it take for you to believe you deserve your desire?

What will it take for you to have faith in yourself or something more, so you achieve your desire?

What will it take for you to believe in your desires or dreams?

How do you feel about what you desire? Excited, fearful, or uncomfortable?

Do you fear having your desire? Why?

Is there a downside to having what you desire? What?

Do you feel you deserve your desire? Why or why not?

If not, what would it take for you to realize you deserve your desires?

Take action to produce my desire

Next, I want you to take some kind of action toward your desires. You can learn more about your desires by joining a group, organization, or do research to get more familiar with it. You can also start using affirmations that include your desires. Always take some kind of action toward your desires, so you can produce results. Larger desires may require more action, along with some persistence. Focus on your desires with the passion they deserve.

What can I do to integrate or accomplish my new desire? What else can I do? What else?

Patiently wait for my desire

It is time to patiently wait for your desire to manifest. Louise Hay speaks to a similar process by using an example of a cosmic kitchen. You have placed your order with intention and confidence knowing what you want. Then, while you sip on your beverage, you can visualize what you desire, as you wait for your order to be prepared. You don't have to worry, question, or doubt if your order is coming.

You believe it will arrive once it is done because you took action by placing your order. Now, you wait on your order, knowing you have taken steps and are deserving of receiving it. Eventually, your desire is delivered, maybe even with a little something extra or better. Now is the time to enjoy what you ordered with appreciation and gratitude. If your order isn't quite what you want, don't get angry or do nothing, simply tell your server in detail what you do want and wait patiently again for your desire to manifest.

Note: The same self-sabotaging obstacles that I talk about earlier in the previous chapters can hinder your desire as well. Stay alert and address any self-sabotaging thoughts, beliefs, and behaviors. Hold on to your desires, and don't let others deter you or degrade them. You don't need anyone else's approval to pursue your personal desires; the only approval you need is your own.

Focus

Focusing on the possibilities of what you are passionate about and how it can be a part of your life can ultimately produce what you desire. This is how manifestation and the law of attraction work: what you focus on is what you create more of.

How do you think other people in the world obtain their personal desires? I guarantee you the people creating their desires are putting an enormous amount of thought, passion, focus, and action into their desires, even if it doesn't look like they are. Great athletes, musicians, business people, moms, and successful entrepreneurs all put an enormous amount of time and energy into their craft.

One of my desires was to have healthy relationships with healthy people. When I was in my mid-twenties, I knew I didn't want any more abusive men or people in my life. Unfortunately, when I focused on *NOT* wanting those kinds of people in my life, that is exactly what I attracted: abusive people and unhealthy relationships. I had to learn to lose the don'ts and shouldn'ts in the descriptions of what I wanted. I changed the way I described my desires. I discovered the best place to start is with the opposite, of what I don't want. For me, that meant I didn't want people in my life that were abusive, selfish, uncaring, or inconsiderate. I needed the opposite of those personality traits: healthy people who were caring, compassionate, and considerate. I took my old list of don't and made a list of positive behavior I desired.

My old list:	**My new list:** (lose the don'ts)
I don't want a man who is abusive.	I want a kind man.
I don't want a man who is inconsiderate.	I want a man who is considerate.
I don't want a man who is selfish.	I want a man who is giving.
I don't want a man who is uncaring.	I want a man who is caring.

Over time, I remained focused and true to my list of what I needed and desired. Eventually, I met my second husband, David. He was kind, considerate, giving, and caring. He treated me with love and respect. He was everything I needed and desired at that point in my life. I will always be grateful for the time we had together.

We all have this powerful tool called focus that can produce wonderful things or our biggest challenges. It all comes down to what you focus on, desires, or challenges. Start focusing on your desires and what you want more of in your life. Let go of what you don't want.

Focus Exercise

The goal is to focus on your desires, physical and emotional needs.

For two weeks, I want you to focus on one of your emotional needs or desires three times a day, similar to how you focused on your affirmations in chapter 4. Once each day, I want you to take time to imagine your desire in your mind with as much detail as possible for at least three minutes.

Definition

Instinct: A largely inherent and unalterable tendency to make a complex and specific response to environmental stimuli without involving reason.

Intuition: Quick and ready insight; the power or faculty of attaining direct knowledge or cognition without evident rational thought and inference.

Flow: A smooth uninterrupted movement or progress.

It's not necessary, but it is much easier to create your desires when you follow your intuition, instinct, and learn to live in flow. These three things can expedite the manifestation process with ease and momentum.

Intuition

I feel our creator has a way of leading us in the right direction. If you want to manifest your desires, you may want to pay attention to coincidences, chance meetings, and especially your own intuition. These kinds of things could be signs leading you toward something special or away from something you don't need or want.

Your inner-knowing is constantly speaking to you while guiding you. Are you watching and listening? Your goal is to see, hear, and feel those messages - even the little ones. There are three things you want to do when letting your intuition take the lead:

1. Pay attention to your situations and the people around you so you can see opportunities or danger.

2. Listen to your intuition or gut first and your mind second. Your gut knows what is best for you. Your mind is a support system to help you get there.

3. Learning to trust in something bigger than yourself, this will lead you in the right direction while taking care of you along the way.

There is a difference between old behaviors, reactions, and gut instinct or intuition. Your gut will never lead you to something that is dangerous or unhealthy. It will try to warn you when something is bad for you or when danger is near. If you are drawn to danger and unhealthy behaviors, recognize that this is more than likely old patterns or behaviors from your past. You may need to go back to evaluate your past beliefs or old behaviors. You can use the inner child recall exercise to discover where and when this behavior started. Here are some questions to help you get in touch with your intuition:

When was the last time I recognized my intuition telling me something? What was it?

When was the last time I paid attention to a coincidence in my life? What was it?

When was the last time someone or something showed up that I had been thinking about?

When have I heard a song or seen an image over and over again that spoke to me?

When have I seen signs or pictures that remind me of something or someone? Then that person calls or shows up.

Have I ever just known things and have no idea why?

Have I ever had a gut feeling that I should do something, and I don't, only to realize it would have been beneficial if I had?

Have I ever had a gut feeling that I shouldn't do something, and I did, only to find myself in trouble? Or I didn't do something and later I find out something bad happened?

Have I ever seen obstacles as signs to do something different?

What would it take for me to become more aware of how the world is guiding me?

There are always signs if you are willing to pay attention. For me, coincidences are a form of guidance, and déjà vu is a way of letting you know you are headed in the right direction.

Flow

The meaning of flow is to move or proceed smoothly and readily. This can be letting life happen so it can guide us in the right direction, being in the right place at the right time or recognizing when to try something different.

Have you ever considered that challenges, obstacles, and detours could be a form of guidance or lessons? Instead of thinking things are going wrong, try to consider it might just be a way of getting you to focus on something different that may actually be better. If you remain patient, you might even see the lesson behind what may have seemed unfair or unjust.

Learn to surrender to faith so positive outcomes are what you receive. When you surrender to flow, life will more than likely work out for the better; when it doesn't, you'll gain knowledge and experience.

I feel it is possible for anyone to live in flow, but it requires patience, tolerance, and acceptance on many levels. The secret is to let go and stop trying to control everyone and everything. There is a reason you don't fight the current of a river; it's much easier to paddle downstream. If you find yourself paddling upstream in the river of life, get out and take a break. After you've caught your breath, you can think clearly and choose to change directions or do something entirely different. Fighting the river, or your life will only cause doubt and frustration that can consume your thoughts and discredit your beliefs.

Have you ever experienced events happening effortlessly or falling into place in your life?

Have you ever known when to take a chance and as a result, things worked out?

Have you ever chosen to stop resisting an impending situation and everything worked out for the better?

Note: If you face intense resistance, it may be an indication that you are not on the right path or living in flow, resistance can provide a chance to change directions, do something different or learn something. When resistance shows up, stay strong and flexible so you can move through it with grace and ease.

Example of living out of flow: Have you ever felt like the more you try to force your life in one direction, the more the world fights back. Have you found yourself trying to make things happen only to face one obstacle after another? Sometimes, what you think you need isn't necessarily what is best for you. Living in flow is all about having faith while trusting that everything is as it should be, and your situation will work out better.

One of my biggest battles with flow, was in my mid-twenties. I was struggling to keep my home after my divorce from my first husband. It seemed like every time things would improve I would suddenly get sick or take two steps backward. I hardly ever had enough money to pay my bills, and I owed more on my home than it was worth. Once I made the decision to let go of my house and move forward with my life, everything started to fall into place. I restructured my finances, I accepted a better job across town, and I found a small affordable place to rent near my new job. Once I quit fighting, moved into flow, let go of my house and literally moved, everything changed, my life started improving, and my desires started rapidly appearing.

The reality was if I hadn't divorced my first husband and eventually given up my home, I may have never met my second husband or gained some distance from my old, unhealthy life. Once I stepped into flow, I discovered more about myself, started obtaining some of my desires, let go of my past, and literally moved forward in a better direction.

REFLECTIONS

- When have I experienced flow in my life?
- When have I changed directions because of resistance?
- What will it take for me to learn how to be more flexible?

When you fight the world, the world will fight back. When you live in flow, the world works with you and provides what you need so you can produce a more balanced, healthier life. Work toward finding your own flow. It will bring you closer to your desires and dreams.

"We all have to stay present today, but it is good to dream of what can be tomorrow!"

Actions to Create Your Desires

Small, daily actions are the secret to successfully manifesting your desires. Remember, you didn't get to this point in your life in just one day, it took months, probably years. Stay focused and diligent as you move forward with these steps:

1. Keep a small place in your thoughts and heart for your desires while staying present in your day-to-day life.

2. Set an intention for your desire every morning while maintaining a belief that you deserve them. Then, throughout the day, act as if your desire has already happened.

   Note: Adopt a "fake it 'till you make it" attitude while manifesting your desire. Incorporate little actions into your life as if you have already produced your desires.

3. Take some kind of action toward your desire every day. Here are a few phrases to use along with your affirmations while creating your desires:

   "Make it happen!"

   "Just do it!"

   "Getter done!"

   "Never give up!"

   "Never give in!"

4. End each day by visualizing and/or listening to your desire. You can look at your magic book (something that I will describe later in this chapter) or imagine yourself having your desire. Listen to my "Hope and Healing" audio every night just before bed or as you go to sleep.

Below are several ways that you can take action in order to create your desires. Once you read through each activity, determine which best fit your personality. You don't need to do every activity, just the ones you connect with.

Clarity Exercise

Go to your *Finding Your Voice* workbook and write down your desire in the center of the page.

1. Close your eyes and imagine what your desire looks, feels, and sounds like.

2. Open your eyes and write down as many words as you can to describe your thoughts. Don't think – just write down each word that comes to mind.

3. Close your eyes again and repeat the process three more times.

4. Go through each word on your page and combine words that mean the same thing.

5. Write down your descriptions of your desire so you can use all of them that are applicable in the following exercises.

Repeat for each of your desires.

Read Your Desires

If you are the type of person that absorbs information through reading, you will want to write down your desires by describing them in the form of an affirmation.

1. Write each affirming statement with the descriptions from the clarity exercise above.

2. Each affirming statement needs to be read every day.

3. You can put them on your mirror or use sticky notes somewhere you will see them frequently. It a great idea to read and reaffirm your desires every night before bed. Don't forget to use wording that you accept and believe.

You can also make a notebook full of your desire statements or write a story in first person that contains all of your desires.

Hear Your Desires

For auditory processors, it's best to hear your desires said out loud. You'll want to focus on, saying affirmation statements to yourself during the day or before bed. One of your best tools may be the mirror exercise for affirmations in chapter four or the *Finding Your Voice* Healing audio on my website: mannettemorgan.com

Visualize Your Desires

If you were one of those children that daydreamed all the time, you are probably a more visual person. Use your imagination to create a picture of your desires with as much detail as you can in your mind, and then you can produce it in your reality. This is very similar to the **SITT PATIENTLY** section in this chapter. The Guided Visualization Meditation practice in the *Finding Your Voice* workbook might be a good fit for you.

1. Create a detailed picture of your desires using some descriptions from the clarity exercise above.

2. When you picture your desires, put yourself in the picture. See yourself living your desire. Learn to become fully immersed in your imagination.

3. Create scenarios in which you receive validation for achieving your desire. Within your imagination, hear and see people congratulate you for your accomplishments.

4. Make your picture as clear and defined as possible.

The goal is to see and feel the experience, which convinces your subconscious you are living your desire.

Other forms of visualization are making a vision board, magic book, or mind movie. These items are a great way to visually see your desires in a physical form:

- A vision board is a poster board that has pictures and words that demonstrate and describe your desires. You can cut your pictures and words out of a magazine, or you can draw and write them if you are more of an artistic type. The project can be a collage or structured – whatever suits you.

- A magic book is a notebook or memory book made up of pictures and words that demonstrate and describe your desires. It is similar to a vision board, but instead, it's in book form. You can have a separate page for different desires. My magic book has different sections divided up into family, health, travel, home, and career.

- Mind movies are videos you can create on a digital device and watch anytime you want to remind yourself of your desires. It is a digital vision board. Check out this website for more information: www.mindmovie.com

I made my first magic book in my early twenties the idea came to me when a friend shared the concept of a vision board. At the time, I didn't have enough money to buy a poster board, so I took an old plastic purple notebook and some notebook paper and made a vision notebook (magic book). I took a piece of notebook paper, put my name in the center of the page and named it Mannette Morgan's New Life. On the next page, I made a list of what I wanted in my new life after leaving my husband.

My List:

I want financial security.

I want someone to love me.

I want to be happy.

I want to travel.

I want a career I like that can support my children and me.

Next, I took every magazine in my house and cut out pictures of things I liked. I cut out pictures of couples holding hands on the beach and on cruise ships. I cut out pictures of interiors and exteriors of houses. I cut out pictures of clothes and jewelry I liked. My magic book was pretty basic, but my desires for my new life were very real. I would look at it each week to remind myself of what I wanted. Once I started dating, I decided to make a list of what I wanted in a partner – I referred to this previously in the focus portion of this chapter – and put those things in my vision book, too. Nothing big happened right away – or at least I didn't think so – but little changes did occur. I continued to go back to my vision book and put new things in it over the next year.

As my life improved, I forgot about my book until twelve years later, when I was moving from Colorado to Singapore, and I found it. When I looked through it, I realized how many things in my book had actually manifested. By this time, I was financially secure; I had been married to two different men who were caring and loved me wholeheartedly; I'd been on more than four cruises with my second husband and was now moving to a tropical country with my third husband. The log house I was moving from looked similar to a house I had in my book, as well as my previous home. I had a design business that supported my family and me. I couldn't believe how many things in my vision book had actually manifested over the previous twelve years. I told my daughter, "I'm going to make a new book, but this time, I'm going to call it my magic book." I also encouraged her to make her own, since she was getting ready to start college and transcend into adulthood. At first, she wasn't too interested, but she eventually made her own magic book. She is 28 now, and she is a master of manifesting her life's desires.

I made my magic book several months after I arrived in Singapore, and I reaped many of the rewards I desired throughout my new magic book. My wish for you is to hold on to your dreams so you can have the life you desire.

Feel Your Desires

Every desire needs to have a positive feeling associated with it. If your desire makes you feel upset, scared, or extremely uncomfortable, you might still be holding on to a past belief that you are unworthy of your desire. Go back to the inner child recall exercises in chapter four. Find out why you feel the way you do about your desire so you can let go of any old beliefs and move forward. It is vital that you feel passion and excitement for your desires.

Take any description from the clarity exercise that has a feeling attached and proceed.

1. Start by associating an intense feeling with each description.

2. Next, close your eyes and focus intently on how you feel as you associate with your desire. (excited, happy, etc.)

3. Sit and immerse yourself with your feelings for three minutes or more if possible.

4. Now open your eyes and take a deep breath. Try to hold on to that feeling throughout your day.

Try using one of the meditation exercises in the *Finding Your Voice* workbook so you can immerse yourself in your feelings or imagination.

Value of Meditation

Meditation comes in all forms, and this isn't just for the new age movement, followers of metaphysics or yogis of this world. Meditation means to engage in contemplation, reflection, or a mental exercise while building a relationship with yourself. There are multiple ways you can meditate: walking, gardening, cooking, or the traditional way of sitting quietly and concentrating on your breath. Meditation can be extremely beneficial – both while you heal and throughout your life.

I have meditated from the time I was 12 when my anxiety issues had become overwhelming. My mom sent me to a hypnotherapist in hopes of lowering my anxiety; she wasn't aware of my sexual abuse at the time. After several sessions with the hypnotherapist, I used the relaxation and self-hypnosis to calm myself on a regular basis. That is when my personal meditation practice started.

I started learning more about traditional meditation in my early twenties. I tried different positions and methods for months before I found what worked for me. In the beginning, I tried the traditional way of sitting cross-legged with my eyes closed, while attempting to empty my mind; that didn't work in the beginning. Then I tried lying down flat on my back while I relaxed deeply, but I would always fall asleep. That shouldn't have been surprising, I had two small children, and I was constantly sleep-deprived. The best way for me to let myself totally relax while remaining in a slightly awakened state was by lying on my back with my knees bent. In time, I discovered how to slow my mind down and connect with stillness.

I would start a practice on Sunday night, and by Wednesday, I couldn't seem to find the five to ten minutes I needed to continue my practice. Then I would give up until the next Sunday or Monday and repeat the process again. Yet, even meditating one to three days per week started helping me feel calmer. Over time, my practice became more consistent while always having some gaps. It was years before I realized I could meditate while I did other things – like walking in nature, gardening, or taking my nightly bath. The key was finding an opportunity to practice stillness and silence.

To this day, I practice meditation. Sometimes my life gets busy, and I don't devote the time I would like to, but I always come back to it. The rewards of meditation for me personally can't be replaced by anything else. It gives me peace, comfort, gratitude, resilience, and a connection to something more. It helps me let go of everything that doesn't truly concern me, so I can ultimately stay present in what *does* concern me. Simply put, it is a gift I give to myself, so I can continue to live in the here and now, fully present and aware.

The first goal to meditation is to quiet your mind and ultimately find that inner peace between your thoughts. You don't need to take hours to practice meditation, just a few moments a day will do. I have listed below some basic information and different types of meditations I have used throughout the years. You can find what best suits you, your personality, and your lifestyle.

- Consider setting an intention before you meditate. Here are a few ideas: discover more love for yourself, find calmness in your life; find more patience, grace, or kindness; create your desires. There is no right or wrong intention; it's all about starting with a desire.

- Meditation is about being present and aware of your own thoughts while letting them come and go. Don't silence your thoughts, recognize each one, and let it pass. It's like watching clouds move across the sky. They are constantly moving and changing. The goal is to learn how to let your brain get out of the way so you can connect with your quiet inner self.

- Sunrise and sunset are good times to practice meditation, if possible. There is something calming about the rising and setting of the sun as night transitions to day and day transitions to night. But any time of day can work. The important thing is to just begin a practice and make it a part of your life. I like to meditate in the dark with candles, or outside alone in nature. I feel more at peace in that type of setting. Discover *your* favorite time and setting.

- Meditation sounds also help my meditation practice. I often use my iPod with earbuds. Some of my meditation sounds include soft music, chanting, and vibration sounds with different frequencies. Having beautiful sounds helps me stay focused, and eliminates distractions.

- You can lie down or sit up to practice meditation. I find it is much easier to start a practice lying down flat on your back, but it isn't necessary. Put a small pillow under your knees to relieve any pressure from your lower back and maybe another one under your neck. It is important to be comfortable. If you find you fall asleep while lying down, it's okay. Your body knows what it does or doesn't need so don't forget to listen to it. If you want to stay a bit more alert, keep your knees up and bent. You can even balance them together and separate your feet about 12 inches. This can keep your body somewhat engaged while relaxed enough to meditate. If you continue to fall asleep, change positions. Try sitting on the floor cross-legged or in a chair with your feet flat on the ground. In time, you will discover your own personal meditation position. Keep in mind meditation is a practice and will get easier in time.

- If you have a lot of negative or emotional thoughts while you meditate, don't worry. You may need to get these thoughts and emotions out, especially if you have suppressed these feelings for a long time. Use the inner child recall exercises in chapter four to process your thoughts and emotions. You can use some of the letting go exercises in chapter seven too. Express your feelings and emotions; then attempt to practice your meditation again another time.

Types of Mediation

Below are different types of meditations. I have included detailed step-by-step information for each one in the *Finding Your Voice* workbook. I also have guided meditations available on my website: mannettemorgan.com

Movement Meditation

Creative Meditation

Relaxation Meditation

Visual Meditation

Guided Visualization Meditation

Closing Summary for Chapter Six

Everything in this chapter has been about discovering who you are, what you need, and what you desire. I hope you discovered more about yourself, including what kinds of eggs you like. If not, no worries. You will get there. Soon there will be no one and nothing stopping you from becoming an independent woman who knows what she wants and needs. You can also reach for your dreams and start manifesting your own desires, you deserve it!

Congratulations! You did it! You worked through chapter six of the healing process. By now, your baby is pulling itself up and standing on its own. You may still lose your balance now and then but look how far you have come. You are doing great, and you will continue to grow and learn more about yourself. Let's keep moving forward so you can start walking and even run as you learn to have a life that is full of happiness and joy.

By now, your tree has more than likely developed a strong root system with a sturdy trunk. Your branches are growing and expanding as you discover your individual personality and seek out your desires. In the next chapter, we are going to focus on letting your tree blossom.

REFLECTIONS

- What have I learned about my needs, wants, and desires?
- What have I discovered about my personality?
- What do I desire most in my life?

- How do I respond best – using visual, audio, or feeling techniques?

- How have I incorporated meditation into my life?

Affirmations: Here are a few new affirmation statements you can add to your list as you work through creating your desires. Remember to believe with conviction while omitting any doubt.

I give myself permission to be true to myself.

I love and accept my true personality.

I am ready to receive everything I physically need.

It is safe for me to receive all of my emotional needs.

I am free to live my life and embrace all the things I desire.

I'm in the process of achieving my desires.

I am learning to accept my desires into my life.

I give myself permission to connect with my inner self and find peace.

I am ready to accept a meditation practice into my life.

One-Month Follow-up Questions

After discovering more about yourself, I would like you to reflect on the questions below every month for three months so you can evaluate personal change.

How much more have I discovered about myself after one month?

    1   2   3   4   5   6   7   8   9   10

How much more do I feel I understand my emotional needs after one month?

    1   2   3   4   5   6   7   8   9   10

How much more am I focusing on my desires after one month?

    1   2   3   4   5   6   7   8   9   10

How much more am I meditating after one month?

    1   2   3   4   5   6   7   8   9   10

CHAPTER 7

Embrace Happiness and Joy

● ●

"HUMPTY DUMPTY SAT ON A WALL Humpty Dumpty had a great fall. All the king's horses and all the king's men couldn't put Humpty back together again." As I read this to my children, I had an epiphany. I realized I had taken a hard fall when I was a child – the day I became a victim. I was broken into pieces, namely, fragmented emotions. All my bits became displaced, for years, I struggled to put myself back together.

In the beginning, only a few pieces fit. The more I discovered about myself and my feelings, the more I began to repair my brokenness. When I learned to let go of my shame, fear, worry, and anger, more of me began to mend and heal. In time, I became whole once again, and I embraced more joy as my tree began to blossom.

By now your tree has taken shape and grown. I'm sure your roots are reaching deep into

197

the earth as you acquire more love and respect for yourself. Your trunk is becoming more stable as you embrace your new beliefs and behaviors. Now your branches are reaching outward while new ones emerge as you discover and reach for your desires. Let's start to nourish those blossoms with sunlight so you can shine with happiness and joy for the world to see.

"Happiness is a choice,
while joy is how I perceive each moment."

To me, happiness is pleasure and contentment that I choose to embrace within myself. Joy is living in the moment while embracing each positive experience. I'm not going to lie to you; it's much easier for some people to experience happiness and joyfulness than others. Some people are born with a 'glass half-full' attitude, and others are born with a 'glass half-empty' outlook. I happen to be one of those people that see life as a pretty full glass. I'm sure some of you are thinking, 'That's why she was able to make all these changes and see the positive side of life.' You might be right, but I feel everyone has the ability to obtain happiness and joy in their own lives. If you are a glass half-full kind of person, this will be easier, but if you aren't, it can still be done. It will just require a little more awareness and deliberate thought on your part.

Do you choose happiness and joy in your life, or not?

I could have given up years ago when things went badly, but I didn't. I chose happiness and a bit of joy, even in my darkest times. That doesn't mean I live a life of extreme happiness and joy 24/7. It just means I maintain a constant emotional state of contentment, with times of joy. I also experience challenges and obstacles, just like you. At times I deal with challenges that have me questioning my own optimism. Then I realize it's my choice how I choose to perceive the world, my challenges, and what I learn for them.

Perception is how we see ourselves, others, and the world as a whole. When you look at the world, what do you see? Do you see doom and gloom, or do you see potential and hope? Beauty is in the eye of the beholder, how do you see in yourself, others and the world. Here are a few statements to assess how you see yourself and the world.

Which sounds more like you?

- "OMG! I am fifty years old! What happened to my body and mind?" Or, "I'm fifty years old, and I'm still hanging in here." Or, "I'm fiftey years old. Look what I've accomplished."

- "That lady is a bitch and out of control. What is her problem?" Or, "That lady must be having a challenging day." Or, "That lady must be struggling. I wish her the best."

Happiness: A mental or emotional state defined by positive or pleasant emotions; satisfied or content with the quality or standard of.

Joy: The emotion evoked by well-being, success, good fortune, or by the prospect of possessing what one desires. A feeling of great pleasure.

I feel our happiness comes from within, not from others. You will likely be disappointed often, if you base your happiness on others and their actions. To me, joy is all about experiencing life as it happens, and learning to embrace each special moment. Strive to discover the happiness and joy within yourself and your life.

Discover Your Happiness and Joy

Ask yourself the following questions and document your answers:

When was the last time I laughed?

When was the last time I laughed until I cried?

When was the last time I felt full of joy or pleasure?

When was the last time I smiled from my heart?

When was the last time I was so happy I cried?

When was the last time I had fun?

When was the last time I felt content?

What is the funniest thing I can remember?

Ask the follow-up questions for each answer above.

Where were you when you felt this way?

What were you doing or thinking?

For the next week, your goal is to incorporate one of these experiences into your daily life.

This exercise is the first step to helping you understand what happiness and joy look, sound, and feel like for you. The positive energy we get from these emotions heals our past while keeping us content in our present moment. I feel that joy can heal your heart, mind, body, and soul.

The following are examples of what happiness and joy look like for me: Take a moment and ask yourself the same questions below and document your answers in your *Finding Your Voice* workbook.

Happiness	When	Accomplishing a small task.
	Where	Being in or near my home.
	What	Relaxing or working on a project.
Joy	When	Dancing, spending time talking and getting know to others.
	Where	Anywhere I am comfortable.
	What	Sharing my thoughts or learning something new.

The happy activities following are the foundation for your new happiness behaviors. One of my favorite books on happiness is *Happy for No Reason* by Marci Shimoff. Some of my happiness activities are very similar to her research. When I read her book, it just reaffirmed most of the beliefs and practices I have embraced for years, some without even being aware of them.

Happiness Boosters

Below is a list of the eight Happy Boosters. Write them all on several cards and put one card in your purse, and one on your favorite mirror or anywhere else you think you're likely to see it daily. When you choose to start living by these small activities in your day-to-day life, your life will change for the better.

Live in the Moment

Take Care of Yourself

Accept & Love Yourself

Accept Others & Give Back to the World

Express Gratitude

Appreciate all Your Experiences

Make time For Your Desires

Give Yourself a Break!

Eight-Week Progressive Exercises

Read through the following definitions for each Happy Booster listed above. I have included an exercise for you to do each week, over eight weeks. Record your progress in your *Finding Your Voice* workbook until you have completed all eight exercises.

"All we truly have is now and in each now is where you will find your own joy and happiness."

Live in the Moment

Live in the moment and learn to be totally present at all times so you can participate fully today. This can be one of our biggest challenges as survivors. Don't waste time on the guilt and shame of yesterday. Likewise, don't let worry and fear of tomorrow overwhelm you today.

When we are present, we can take in life's moments of joy as they happen. Have you ever observed young children playing? They are totally immersed in their activity - until they learn not to be. If you learn to live in the now, you won't experience as much regret or feel quite as guilty tomorrow. Only by being present can you experience all the great moments you might be missing.

Live in the Moment Exercise

Week one, write down how many times a day you were totally present while experiencing life. This can include thoughts, actions, activities, events, interactions, or being in nature.

How present am I in my own life?

Do I ever truly immerse myself in nature?

Do I ever immerse myself in what I'm doing?

203

Am I truly present when I'm with others?

How much have I been missing?

Take Care of Yourself

Make time to take care of your emotional, mental, and physical well-being every day while treating yourself with kindness and respect.

Start incorporating a healthy daily routine into your life. It can be eating something you like that is good for you, exercising, taking walks or reserving quiet time for yourself. Learn something new or try something you have always had a desire to do. Reap the rewards of feeling satisfied and happy for accomplishing something daily, even if it is a small task. Accomplishment and satisfaction produce a sense of happiness and fulfillment.

You can also create an environment that is relaxing and comfortable. Organize your life, office, or home by decluttering. This can give you a sense of accomplishment while decreasing the chaos in your life. Then surround yourself with things you love or that have personal meaning to you.

Taking Care of Yourself Exercise

Week two, start a meditation practice for five minutes a day or consider starting a healthy exercise or nutrition routine. You could also try yoga or spending time in nature.

Over the next week don't try to take on the world. Just make one change and make it count. Remember it is all about what you *can* do – not what you *should* do. Treat yourself like you would your best friend if she was taking on a new practice of some kind. Recognize all of your accomplishments and remember it is a practice not an absolute.

Which practice are you taking on for the next week?

Two-Week Follow-up:
How much calmer or more at ease do you feel?
How much better do you feel about yourself?
How many times did you smile this week when you completed your practice?

Accept and Love Yourself

Happiness is contentment, and contentment comes with self-acceptance and self-love. Both components are a vital part of happiness. If you have already conquered learning how to accept and love yourself, great! You'll have a light week, if not keep at it.

Self-Acceptance Exercise

Week three, convert any old negative thoughts, actions, and experiences into something more positive. You can refer back to The Big 3 if you are still struggling with self-acceptance and self-love.

How am I talking to myself?

Am I still using negative self-talk?

What am I saying?

If so, what positive thought or expression am I going to replace it with?

At the end of week three, how much more content do I feel?

"The smallest kind gesture can change the world and then become contagious."

Accept Others and Give Back to the World

Practice acceptance and forgiveness for the people you love and let them live their lives the way they choose. Search for the positive uniqueness in everyone, while unconditionally accepting them along with their imperfections.

Make it a practice to smile, lend a helping hand, or donate time or money. Send someone you love a kind text or a loving note to let them know you care. When you do something for someone else, you are giving yourself a gift as well as them. Our lives are about giving and receiving. Be proud of your ability to give, and enjoy receiving, the emotional rewards in return.

While doing your best to be kind to others, they may not reciprocate the way you think they should, let it go and move on. Know in your own heart you were kind in your actions. This is why it is called a *gift*; remember, not all gifts are acknowledged or reciprocated.

I always say we never know what goes on behind closed doors or what someone else is going through. It's important to accept and forgive others, excluding abusive behavior. Learn to let go of expectations and judgment. Accept each individual for who they are – nothing more, nothing less and learn not to take others' reactions personally; it isn't always about you.

Accepting Others and Giving Exercise

In week four, I want you to smile at a stranger, give a compliment, or hold the door open for someone. Write down how many times you did something kind for someone else.

What did I do for someone else today?

How many people responded positively to my action?

How much better did I feel after one week of giving gifts to the world?

Note: When doing kind gestures for others, this doesn't mean you neglect yourself.

Express Gratitude

Express gratitude for everything around you, especially the small things. Learn to recognize all the beauty in the world and give thanks for it: a tree, bird, flower, or the bright blue sky. Find the beauty in children's expressions, actions, and especially the quirky things they do. Discover the beauty in your family, friends, pets, and everything that surrounds you.

Everyone and everything offers something special if we are willing to see it. Find gratitude for what you already have and what you have accomplished. Don't waste time and energy focusing on what you don't have. There is always something to be grateful for.

Gratitude Exercise

Week five write down five things you are grateful for each night before bed and give thanks for those things. You will begin to see that there is more beauty when you focus on the possibilities.

What five things am I grateful for today?

Did I discover something I was grateful for, that I wasn't aware of?

How much lighter and more content do I feel after week five?

"Don't get lost in what's next or what could have been.
You might miss out on what is."

Appreciate All Your Experiences

Learn to appreciate each experience as it happens. Don't get lost in what's next or what could have been. You might miss out on what is. The more positive experiences we choose to participate in the more joy, love, and happiness we will obtain.

Some of our daily experiences are fun and exciting; some are challenging. There is always something to take away from each experience from joy or excitement to disappointment or anguish. Most of your negative experiences can possess a lesson, especially the hardest and most challenging ones. Your job is to learn how to recognize and embrace the underlining lesson. Sometimes we don't always see the lesson initially, but eventually, we can ultimately understand.

I remember my early twenties when I felt like my life was falling apart. My husband and best friend were having an affair, and I felt like I was losing my mind and everyone around me. I couldn't see the lessons in front of me; all I could do was just get through each day. Eventually, I separated from both my husband and best friend. It took time for me to see the lesson that I needed to let go of my destructive relationships and find healthier relationships. Eventually, over time, I became grateful to both of them. Their relationship forced me to make a choice to leave, so I could ultimately make better decisions for myself and obtain a happier life.

Experiences Exercise

Week six, take your *Finding Your Voice* workbook and make a note of how you felt during one of your most positive experiences in life.

Did I immerse myself in my experience?

Did I experience joy, happiness, or excitement?

How can I recreate a similar experience in the near future?

You can take this exercise further and evaluate past challenging life experiences as you look for the underlining lessons.

Finding Your Voice

REFLECTIONS

- What can I learn from one of my past experiences? Anything else?

- How did that experience change my life?

- How do I relate to my experience today?

Make Time for Your Desires

Work on incorporating your desires and passions into your hobbies, free time, work, or life. You deserve the feeling of joy and elation that comes with living your passions. Experiencing these feelings releases endorphins that create a natural high and a state of joy. If you have already started incorporating your desires and passions, great! This week will be easy.

Desire and Passion Exercise

Week seven, write down and start incorporating a desire and/or passion into your life.

Which desire or passion am I going to integrate into my life?

How am I going to integrate my desire or passion into my life this week?

How did I feel after integrating my desire or passion at the end of week seven?

Give Yourself a Break

If you managed to accomplish all your new happiness activities in seven weeks, congratulations! You might be wonder woman. If you are still getting there, give yourself a break. We are all human, and no one is perfect. The effort you are putting into this work will change your life so you can obtain more happiness and joy. Please don't give up. Your happiness and joy are within reach.

Sometimes we all just need to stop or pause. When you hit the brakes, reflect on how much you have changed and what you have learned as you give yourself time and space.

Break Exercise

During week eight, it is time to take a break and reward yourself for all the work you have done up to this point and reflect on what you have achieved. Treat yourself to something special for cultivating your new relationship with happiness. Be grateful for what you have accomplished and how you see life differently now.

After eight weeks, do I feel differently about the world?

Do I feel happier and more at peace?

Am I experiencing more joy?

Has anyone I know noticed that I seem different, maybe even happier?

"I looked up, down and all around, but when I looked inside,
I found myself."

The Happy Busters

Let me introduce you to the Happy Busters. Guilt, shame, fear, worry, anxiety, and anger can hold you emotionally hostage and limit your happiness potential. As a survivor, it's possible you are holding on to one or more of these Happy Busters. One or all of these Happy busters can sabotage the work you have done up to this point. So, if you are still struggling to find acceptance, happiness, self-love, joy, peace or self-respect, one or all of these six Happy Busters could be preventing you from healing.

Are you aware of how much guilt, shame, fear, worry, anxiety, and anger you possess?

If you learned to feel ashamed as a child, you will more than likely carry your shame throughout your adulthood. If you learned how to worry from one of your parents, you likely worry to this day. We are all capable of carrying these emotions from childhood into adulthood.

REFLECTIONS

Which of these emotions do you want to experience going forward?

Guilt	or	Acceptance and Forgiveness
Shame	or	Self-respect
Fear	or	Faith and Confidence
Worry	or	Happiness
Anxiety	or	Peace
Anger	or	Compassion and Expression

Happy Busters can consume our lives while depleting our happiness, joy, and passion. If you want to experience more happiness and joy, it would benefit you to tame or even let go of these challenging emotions. To do this, you will need to reprogram the thoughts you've acquired throughout the years. Here are a few thoughts to consider for each emotion.

If you choose to live with. . .

Guilt, you will more than likely live a life full of self-criticism and doubt.

Shame, you will live a life full of disrespect and low self-worth.

Fear, you will live a life full of panic and anxiety.

Worry, you will live a life full of crisis and tragedy.

Anxiety, you will live a life full of stress and discomfort.

Anger, you will live a life full of obstacles and resistance.

You could choose to live a life without. . .

Guilt, so you can gain love and acceptance for yourself.

Shame, so you can gain self-worth and self-respect.

Fears, so you can gain confidence and faith while feeling safe and secure.

Worry, so you can gain more happiness, joy, contentment, and abundance.

Anxiety, so you can gain peace and serenity.

Anger, so you can gain tolerance and compassion for yourself and others.

I have broken the *Happy Busters* up into three sections: First, we will discuss guilt and shame as well as how to heal these through forgiveness. Second, we will discuss fear, worry, and anxiety. Finally, we will dive into anger and how it can keep you from obtaining happiness.

Guilt and Shame

Guilt: An emotion that occurs when a person believes that they have violated a moral standard they believe in. It is also a sense of deserving to be blamed, especially for imagined offenses or from a sense of inadequacy. I committed or performed a behavior or action that offended my own belief.

Shame: A painful emotion caused by the consciousness of guilt, shortcoming, or impropriety; it is a feeling of regret or embarrassment or a sense of having been dishonored or disgraced. I am _____ (bad, less than, horrible, etc.).

Forgiveness: To cease to feel resentment against an offender. Forgiveness entails no longer resenting, blaming or anger toward oneself or others for a wrong.

Guilt

Guilt can be a constructive emotion that ultimately keeps us in check and helps us uphold our own moral standards, or it can be a belief we are deserving of blame and are inadequate. Another form of guilt is taking on the responsibility of other people's issues or challenges when they don't really involve us.

Guilt can be cultivated and learned from childhood or reinforced through abuse. Abusers can create a manipulative environment in order to control or gain power over a victim. Some people may impose guilt in order to solicit certain reactions from others. They may behave this way because they lack self-confidence, are fearful of losing control, or are dealing with unmet needs. Some individuals use passive-aggressive behavior to control others and guilt them into submission. Most of the time, these behaviors aren't even about you; it's usually about them.

 REFLECTIONS

- What kind of guilt have you experienced?
- Have I felt guilty because I have violated a personal moral standard?
- Have I felt guilty for something that doesn't really pertain to me?
- Have I known someone that uses guilt to get what they need?
- Have I been made to feel guilty because of someone else insecurities?
- Have I been made to feel guilty by someone that wants to control me?
- Is my guilt mine, or is it someone else's burden I choose to carry?
- Have I used guilt to get something I need?

If you feel guilty about a behavior or action that you feel is unjust or wrong, make a point to apologize for your behavior. The person you apologize to can choose to accept your apology or not. No matter the outcome, you have to choose to let your guilt go once you have done what you can to mend the situation.

The word *n,o* and the guilt that comes with it can be another challenge. *No* is a powerful and necessary word. You have the right to use the word *no*, even if you were brought up in an environment that didn't allow it or respect your voice. Our inability to use the word *no* could have caused challenges for us throughout the years. It's actually an appropriate word when you don't want to engage or participate. There is really no need to explain yourself or make excuses. Know who you are, be strong, and learn to say *no* with kindness and without guilt.

If others don't accept the word no or try to guilt you into submission, consider strengthening your boundaries in those relationships. Once you reach a point of self-respect, it's much easier not let others imprint guilt on you.

Are you one of those people who say "I'm sorry" to everyone constantly? That would be my role throughout the years, and it screams guilt. When you learn to accept and respect yourself, you can learn to let go of the apologies and the guilt that goes with it. Unfortunately, you may have developed a habit/pattern which requires changing your behavior if so, use the reprogramming exercises in chapter five.

Has my use of *"I'm sorry"* become a habit?

Shame

Shame can take our emotions one step further than guilt. Shame is a feeling of regret, embarrassment, and disgrace, as the result of our guilt or shortcomings. Most of us formed this belief during or after our abuse. As a survivor, we can carry the burden of shame, which leads to self-criticism without self-respect. Shame can be self-inflicted or become a projected overlay by our abuser.

Unfortunately, over time, our shame can evolve into humiliation. People who accept humiliation as a belief often become long-term victims as they find themselves ashamed and embarrassed of themselves and their past.

Once you better understand the differences between the three (guilt, shame, and humiliation), you have a choice to accept these beliefs or not. When you learn to find compassion and acceptance for yourself, then you can live a life absent of shame. The ultimate healing component for all of these is forgiveness.

 REFLECTIONS

- Do I carry the burden of shame?
- Has my shame become humiliation?
- Have I found myself re-experiencing old shameful experiences over and over again?
- Have I found myself continuously in abusive relationships, just with different people?

Forgiveness

Forgiveness can be one of the most challenging parts of healing and at the same time, powerful. It can be uncomfortable as it brings up feelings of resentment and even anger toward others and maybe yourself.

There are three major parts to forgiveness: forgiving yourself, forgiving the monster, and forgiving the people who didn't protect you. Hear me out. I'm not saying you have to forgive everyone, but there is likely some work to be done when it comes to forgiveness.

> *"I forgive myself for the wrongs done to me, and I choose to take full responsibility for my life going forward."*

Forgive Yourself

You were a victim of something horrible that changed your life. It's your choice to forgive yourself for any part of the abuse you might feel responsible for. It doesn't matter if you did or didn't do what you thought you should or shouldn't. It doesn't matter if you feel you did something wrong. It doesn't matter if you never said *no* or said *no* a thousand times. It doesn't matter if you ended up feeling a certain amount of pleasure during your abuse. It doesn't matter if you felt obligated or even loved your abuser. None of it really matters! The facts are it happened, and it was abuse.

We all do whatever it takes to survive our experience. Your past abuse doesn't have to define how you feel about yourself today. I want you to consider forgiving yourself for whatever you did or didn't do. You are the only one that can give yourself the gift of *forgiveness*. No one else can do this for you. Please, find compassion and forgiveness for whatever you did to survive and cope.

If you were a child or teenager the first time you experienced abuse, you also want to forgive that child or teenager. If you were a young adult or grown-up when you experienced abuse and you feel you put yourself in a dangerous, risky or careless situation, you need to consider forgiving yourself for whatever part you feel you contributed. We all make mistakes throughout our lives. Don't hold yourself hostage for something you did or didn't do during your abuse.

Remember the abuser/perpetrator is to blame – not you (the victim). Think about it: were you the abuser, or were you the victim? Wrong is wrong. Just because you were young, naive, or vulnerable, doesn't give an abuser the right to take something from you that doesn't belong to them.

Start letting go of decisions, patterns, and events you hold yourself responsible for. If you really want to heal, then it's time to replace shame, hate, resentment, and anger with compassion and self-love. Release those negative feelings and forgive yourself so you can heal and have peace.

Forgive the Monster or Not

I will never ask you to forgive your abuser/perpetrator. I will ask you to accept that they are human and imperfect. Your abuser has their own past, challenges, and demons. Unfortunately, your abuser has probably experienced some kind of abuse in his or her own life or at the least witnessed it. Every behavior is learned – from acceptance to racism, kindness to abuse. People who have experienced abuse usually become a victim or an abuser, which in turn creates a cycle of abuse.

Ignorance doesn't excuse abuse, but it can explain why some abusers start these types of behaviors early on. When we have been taught that there is nothing wrong with the abuse that we are experiencing, it can make it hard for us to later understand that our abusive behavior toward another person is wrong. Some abusers can become consumed with unhealthy curiosity or desire because of what they were exposed to earlier in their lives.

However, most abusers know their actions will be seen as wrong by other people, which is why they often feel the need to manipulate, hide, and control their victims. Some abusers just don't want to face their unhealthy, abusive behaviors or addictions; some abusers realize how horrible their actions are, while others, like children who abuse other children, can be unaware that their behaviors are wrong or harmful.

Whichever the case is, they have formed their own behaviors, and now they have to live with the consequences of their choices. Unfortunately, we do too. This doesn't mean we should excuse or accept their behaviors. What they did was unacceptable and inexcusable. I'm asking you to understand that everyone has a past, and we all learn different things from our individual experiences and environments. Sometimes when we understand everyone is flawed, it's easier to find peace for ourselves.

Here are a few questions you can ask yourself about your abuser if you are one of those people that questions *why* as I did. Recognize that you may never receive the answer you are searching for.

 REFLECTIONS

- Where did they learn their abusive behavior?

- What kind of pain have they experienced in their own life?

- Were they a victim before they became an abuser?

- Did they have anyone to protect them, show them healthy behaviors, or teach them right from wrong?

If you still know your abuser, you can try to seek answers or confront them. Confronting isn't for everyone, and I would recommend you have a strong support system as well as a professional therapist before confronting your abuser. If you are a victim who has chosen to be an abuser, please seek help and stop the cycle of abuse.

Note: I don't condone the actions or behaviors of any abusers. Throughout the years, I have learned to find a small amount of compassion for abusers while strongly asserting they should get help and correct their behaviors. In my view, they are missing something within themselves that they are trying to fill by doing such destructive, harmful things to others.

Forgiving Your Protectors

Your parents or family can play quite a few roles in your life when it comes to abuse. They can stand up and protect you, or they can be the abusers. They can be the person who puts their head in the sand and never looks up to see your abuse. They can also be a victim and/or the co-dependent of the abuser. Just because they are parents doesn't mean they are an expert on recognizing or stopping abuse. In fact, they are human just like you, and they are limited by their own knowledge. As I said early in this book, most of our beliefs, behaviors, and information comes from our families and communities early in our lives. My husband always says, "You don't know what you don't know." This is true in so many aspects of our lives, especially parenting.

I'm not going to presume I know what your abusive experience was like. I don't know if your perpetrator was a family member, someone close to your family, a friend, or a complete stranger. I don't know if your family understood abuse or not. I don't know if you tried to tell someone or not. I don't know what you went through or how the people around you reacted to your abuse.

If you were lucky, you had a support system that got you the help you so desperately needed. If not, you may be living with an unhealthy, broken family to this day.

Parents that didn't know: If you grew up in a family that didn't protect you from an abuser because they didn't know, you might want to find a way to forgive them. They didn't have special glasses to see the secrets you were hiding from the world. They couldn't read your mind or know about your abuse if you didn't tell them. Like I said before, none of us can go back and change what we did or didn't do. Please understand no one wants to believe that these kinds of terrible things happen in their own family, home, or among friends. Try to forgive your parents if they didn't know so you can heal and release yourself and them from the burden.

Parents that knew: Sometimes when we try to help the people we love, we don't always do the right thing for them. No matter how horribly your parents may have handled your situation, I want to believe they did the best they could with the knowledge and tools they had at the time. Know that there are always exceptions, and some parents may have known what needed to be done, but they didn't have the strength or courage to do it. I sympathize if that was your experience.

Abusive parents: If one or both of your parents were abusive, I'm so sorry for the pain you experienced. I can't even imagine the pain you survived. To me, this is one of the most horrific situations any child would have to endure. Especially if one of your parents sexually abused you during your childhood and the other parent didn't believe you or stand up for you because they weren't willing to give up a relationship with the abuser. The people you should be able to trust betrayed you and taught you what it truly feels like to be unworthy of acceptance, love, or respect.

Yet even in this situation, there is hope for you. Everyone can learn how to love and respect themselves. The trust and acceptance you seek may take time, but I feel strongly that it can be done. If either of these is your story, I feel forgiveness is all about you forgiving yourself and whatever it took for you to survive and copy.

How to Forgive

Most of the time, the person we struggle to forgive is the one person who needs forgiveness the most: ourselves. Look in the mirror. Do you need to release yourself from guilt or shame? If so, forgive that little girl that was trapped in a horrible situation, she didn't even understand. Forgive that teenager who thought that she could handle anything until a situation arose in which she couldn't. Forgive the young woman that wanted attention and got more attention than she bargained for. Forgive that woman who thought she knew what she wanted and couldn't see the red flags until it was too late. It's time to forgive yourself for whatever happened.

I'm asking you to forgive yourself for:

Thoughts or beliefs that say you caused your abuse.

Beliefs that you had any control over your situation.

Beliefs that you could have changed what happened.

Beliefs that you are a bad person.

Any behaviors you acquired in order to survive.

Let go of your pain, anger, sadness, guilt, shame, and resentment. Find compassion and forgive yourself. It is time to live a life free of pain and full of happiness, with some joy sprinkled in.

As a child, I always felt that if I had just run and told the first time, it would have never happened again. I'll never know. I grew up and became a woman who chose to have relationships full of drama and emotional abuse. Unfortunately, it felt comfortable and normal to me.

First, I learned to understand I was not to blame. I was only a little girl and a victim of incest. Eventually, I forgave myself for all the behaviors I acquired as a survivor. Then I forgave myself for choosing relationships with abusive people.

Second, I forgave my dad for repeating the emotional abuse he learned from his parents.

Third, I forgave my ex-husband for repeating the emotional abuse he learned from his mother.

Finally, I forgave my cousin for the horrific things he chose to do to me.

Once I forgave myself and each one of my abusers. I found myself free of my shame, my pain, and my past.

Understand you may have made mistakes or been involved in situations you didn't like. Let go of those old shameful feelings. Learn from what you have experienced and don't repeat those unhealthy behaviors. Forgive yourself and those you can. Take responsibility for your life and move forward. Live for the now and let go of the past.

Note: If you have the capacity to forgive your abuser for their actions, you are a remarkable person, and I praise you for your compassion and kindness. I realize some abusers are easier to forgive than others, depending on the severity of the abuse. This choice is totally up to you, and no one will think less of you if you can't forgive your abuser.

Healing Past Guilt and Shame

Below is an exercise that can help you deal with your guilt and shame. The exercises throughout the rest of this chapter and in the *Finding Your Voice* workbook are great tools for dealing with Happy Busters. Each exercise is labeled with the individual Happy Buster it applies to.

Take your workbook and make a list of any wrongdoings you feel guilty about to this day. Next, make a list of anything you feel ashamed of. These are things you regret or feel disgraced by. They could also include some of the behaviors you identified in earlier chapters. Then, over the next week, use one of the exercises from this chapter or the *Finding Your Voice* workbook to start healing from your guilt and shame. The following might help you identify your guilt and shame.

Something you regret doing to someone else.

Something you may have done when you were younger.

Something you didn't do, that you wish you would have done.

Any survival skill you regret you did.

Any uncomfortable decisions you made that were necessary to survive your circumstances.

Expel Writing Exercise
(guilt, shame, fear, worry, anxiety, and anger)

Expel means to push or force something out. I want you to push out your old emotions and let them go. This is for you alone, so don't worry about grammar or punctuation, just write. Set a timer for ten minutes, so you don't have to think about when you need to stop. Your job is to regurgitate your experience and feelings onto paper, with as much emotion as possible.

1. First, I want you to write a letter to yourself or whomever you choose for anything you feel guiltily about or ashamed of. The important part of this exercise is to feel and express your emotions. Expel everything onto the pages: confession, disappointment, judgment, distress, etc.

2. Once you're done writing, if your guilt applies directly to you, I want you to go to a mirror and apologize to yourself. Truly apologize and forgive yourself for whatever you have done. If you are still emotional, let it all out and find compassion and understanding for whatever you did, the same way you would empathize with a best friend who was admitting these things to you. Let it out; let it go and forgive.

3. Once you're done, you're done. Now it's time to perform a ritual and let go of all the guilt you've been carrying. I usually have a little ceremony and burn my letters. I say a little prayer and then give it to something bigger than me. While you're burning your letter, make a concerted effort to honestly let it go and forgive yourself or others.

Reactions for Past and Present Guilt:

Take responsibility for your past and present actions (good and bad) as you learn to make healthier decisions. You can choose to repair old wrongdoings by making amends or sincerely apologizing. Not everyone will accept your positive gesture or apology, if you were sincere, that is all you can do. It's time to let go of the situation and move on. They will either forgive you or not.

Reactions for Past and Present Shame:

Don't let shame dominate your life anymore. When shame shows up, use the expel writing exercise and replace those old thoughts and feelings with positive affirmations. It is time to tame your shame and let it go once and for all.

Affirmations for Shame and Forgiveness:

I have felt shame long enough. Now I'm learning to forgive myself.

I am learning to forgive myself with love and compassion.

I forgive myself because I am worthy of forgiveness.

I forgive myself for any wrongs I have done, and I accept that I am human.

I forgive myself and others for the wrongs done to me.

I choose to take full responsibility for my life going forward.

I am learning to forgive others who have hurt me, so I have room for love.

I forgive myself, so I can fill my heart with peace.

I am in the process of forgiving myself, so I can accept more joy into my life.

I am doing my best to be a good person, and my best is always enough.

These two of the six Happy Busters (guilt and shame) have to do with how we perceive ourselves, similar to the Big 3. They can be healed with empathy, compassion, love, acceptance, and most of all, forgiveness for ourselves.

Fear, Worry and Anxiety

Fear: Unpleasant, often strong, emotion caused by anticipation or awareness of danger.

Worry: A mental distress or agitation resulting from concern usually for something impending or anticipated.

Stress: A physical, chemical, or emotional factor that causes bodily or mental tension and may be a factor in disease causation. Stress is usually a result of a reaction in the moment.

Anxiety: An abnormal and overwhelming sense of apprehension and fear often marked by physical signs such as tension, sweating, and increased heart rate.

Fear

Fear always seems to be at the core of worry, stress, and anxiety. All three of these emotions are the result of letting fear dominate your focus and thoughts.

Humans have a tendency to hold on to our fearful experiences and even replay them in our thoughts, which can result in worry, anxiety, or even PTSD (Post Traumatic Stress Disorder). When we allow our lives to become consumed with worry and anxiety – fearful of past trauma – we are depriving ourselves of present experiences and push happiness and joy further away.

Keen awareness and focus on survival are in our genetic makeup from our Neanderthal ancestors; in order to survive, they had to pay attention and learn from any fearful experiences in their environment. We are their descendants, so we are acutely programmed to focus on the negative, fearful experiences in our own lives. Why do you think everyone is so interested in the wreck on the side of the road or the drama in the tabloids? It's because we emotionally respond to fearful events and problematic situations. Fear is still necessary for survival in certain situations; it isn't as imperative as it was thousands of years ago, but it can still play a role in some of our lives today.

Daily news – whether online, in print, or on television – can be stressful for some people. News often contains a lot of negative energy that actually doesn't affect your personal space and experiences, but it can still impact you emotionally. You have a choice of how much or little fear you want to absorb into your daily life. I'm not saying you have to put your head in the sand. There is nothing wrong with being informed, and I realize that there is some valuable information on the news. All I'm saying is you might not want to saturate your environment with negative information 365 days a year.

REFLECTIONS

- How has fear triggered worry or anxiety in my life?
- How many of my thoughts are fear-based?

If you are a person who lives in a constant state of fear, worry, or anxiety, it's vital you learn self-calming techniques that work for you. You also would benefit from understanding the differences between your current fearful situations and old, repetitive, fearful thoughts replaying in your mind.

Worry

"If you spend all your time worrying about the negative 'What ifs' of tomorrow, you aren't focusing on what could be today."

Worry is an attempt to control that which we cannot control. Worry focusses on the unforeseen obstacles that can produce the *"What ifs"* we manifest in our minds. *What ifs* are those dominating concerns that consume our thoughts. *What if ___ happens? What if he or she does ___? What if things go terribly wrong?* Most of us overthink every scenario and imagine the worst possible outcome. Work toward stopping this thought process, we live in the now, not the "doomed" future. Remain present while only considering the facts. Create solutions, not crisis. The more you gain faith in the fact that everything will work out – all is as it should be – the less there is to worry about. Don't let the *"What ifs"* hold you hostage.

If you constantly worry about others and world situations, you only cause yourself anguish. No matter how much thought you put into others or world issues, you cannot change the outcome, unless you are willing to get out there and do something about it. All of your worrying can't change someone's situation or the world. Each individual has to take responsibility for their own life, and no one else can do it for them. If you are the type who chooses to engage in others' issues, you could be playing the role of co-dependent. Instead of co-dependency, another option is to send good thoughts or prayers to others and the world as you fully participate in your own life.

If you are constantly worrying about your family, children, or spouse, guess what? You only have limited control over that too. Let's start with your partner. They are their own person, and no matter how hard you try, you are not going to change or fix them. They have to find their own way in their own time. You are their partner – not their keeper nor their mother.

The same goes for your younger children. We all want the best for our children. We want them to be healthy and happy. You can make sure your children eat well, and they are taken care of. You can provide a stimulating and happy environment, but you can't control the outside influences of the world. In other words, you can't control everything your job is to guide and lead your children into adulthood. Your worry isn't going to change anything only your actions can.

The truth is you are a compassionate, concerned bystander with limited control. I'm suggesting you remain realistic and keep a positive attitude without worry. When it comes to your partner, family and grown children, wish them the best, send them love, help where you can and let them find their own way through their own struggles. Teach and display independence, not co-dependence.

How much worry do I have in my daily life?

1   2   3   4   5   6   7   8   9   10

Answer the questions below. When finished, use one of the letting go exercises in this section or in your *Finding Your Voice* workbook. I personally feel the balloon visualization exercise is great for worry.

REFLECTIONS

- When do I let *what ifs* consume my thoughts?
- What specific *what ifs* am I worrying about?
- Do I have any control over the situations I'm worrying about?
- What can I do to resolve the situation?
- Is the situation I'm worrying about any of my business?
- What else do I continually worry about?

Note: I personally feel worry is a wasted emotion that contains negative thoughts and energy. Think about it. Is there anything worth constant worry? If you can't do anything about it, let it go. If you can, do something about it. It is truly that simple.

Balloon Visual Exercise
(guilt, shame, fear, worry, anxiety, and anger)

After surviving abuse, we sometimes have certain emotions and beliefs that can tether themselves to us. Can you imagine having several balloons attached to your physical body by either strings or with static electricity all day, every day? Imagine each one of those balloons represents a different negative emotion or situation, and you have them attached to you in your car, at your work, when you are trying to play with your children or when you're having an intimate moment with your partner.

These emotions and beliefs can weigh you down as they occupy your thought. Imagine you have a balloon filled with worry and you try to brush it away, only to have it remain attached to you. Can you see how this might be hindering your life?

Let's start by imagining that each challenging emotion or situation has its own balloon. Each one can be a different size, shape, and color. Maybe they take on an image of whatever emotion you feel. Every balloon has something written in or on it that describes what you want to release. Imagine your balloons with as much or as little detail as you wish.

Close your eyes. Imagine one balloon at a time that contains the emotion or situation you want to release. Ask yourself the following questions for each one:

Is this balloon (emotion or situation) any of my business?

Does this balloon belong to me or to someone else?

Release – If this isn't your business or doesn't belong to you, cut the string, let it float away or burst your balloon, let it go, so it finds its way to wherever and whomever it belongs.

Do I have any control over this balloon (emotion or situation) or person?

Is this thought, emotion, or belief completely true?

Release – If you don't have any control or it isn't true cut the string or burst your balloon so you can let it go.

Can I change or fix the situation?

Should I try to change or fix it?

Release – If not, cut the string or burst the balloon so you can let it go.

Action – If you can change the situation and it's your responsibility to change it, take action and do something to change it—responses for each Happy Buster.

- **Guilt:** Make amends or apologize. Take whatever is left, put it in the balloon, burst it, or let it float away.

- **Shame:** Make amends and forgive yourself. Take whatever is left, put it in the balloon, burst it, or let it float away.

- **Fear:** Face it and deal with whatever is threatening. Take what's left, put it in the balloon, burst it, or let it float away.

- **Anxiety:** Use one of the exercises from the anxiety section to calm yourself. Take whatever is left, put it in the balloon, burst it, or let it float away.

- **Worry:** For goodness sakes! Put it in the balloon, burst it, or let it float away.

- **Anger:** Face it or perform an anger exercise. Take whatever is left, put it in the balloon, burst it, or let it float away.

One of the most valuable things you can learn is how to let things go that you cannot change, control, or that don't concern you in the first place. Burst those Happy Buster and let go of those balloons.

How much lighter or freer do I feel after doing this exercise?

1   2   3   4   5   6   7   8   9   10

Stress and Anxiety

Stress is a body's way of reacting to fear-based challenges. Anxiety is an unpleasant state of overwhelming inner turmoil and the result of fear, worry, and uneasiness. Anxiety can be subjective and can be an overreaction to certain situations. Consider the following ideas:

- Fear resulting from worry is a common component of anxiety.

- The unknowns of life are much more frightening and can cause anxiety than the reassurance of knowing what is to come.

- Suppressing our feelings can also result in anxiety.

- The inner turmoil of reliving our traumatic experiences in our dreams or thoughts over and over again can result in post-traumatic stress disorder (PTSD) or uncontrollable anxiety.

- Anger issues and/or overreactions to life events is another cause. Some of us get angry when we feel we are losing control of a situation or when we feel we are backed into a corner, the result can be stress or anxiety.

There are three sources of stress: your environment, your body, and your thoughts. Anxiety and stress can destroy your physical and mental health while making all aspects of your life more challenging.

Symptoms of Stress and Anxiety

Below I have listed the physical symptoms of stress and anxiety. In the *Finding Your Voice* workbook, I have also included the negative emotions that can directly accompany physical ailments. Understanding the correlation between the two can help lower anxiety. Put a check by the symptoms that apply to you.

- Feelings of panic and/or uneasiness
- Irritability, nervousness and/or mood swings
- Muscle discomfort, tension, aches and pains
- Frequent headaches
- Tension in the back of the neck and/or shoulders
- Irregular breathing/hyperventilation
- Stomach discomfort/ulcers, heartburn or Intestinal discomfort
- Tightening and/or tension in the chest, heart palpitations
- Disturbance in sleep habits/insomnia

What are Your Anxiety Accelerators?

Write down your anxiety accelerators in your *Finding Your Voice* workbook.

> Where do you experience stress or anxiety (at work, home, outside your home)?
>
> When do you experience stress or anxiety (morning, day, night, with others or when alone)?
>
> What triggers your stress or anxiety (people, places, or things)?

Make a list of what triggers your anxiety in the first column. Then make a list of how many times a day or week this affects your life.

Stress and Anxiety Triggers   How many times a day or week?
1)
2)
3)

If you're struggling with high levels of anxiety and you don't seem to understand why or where it originated, I suggest you go back and use the inner child recall exercise to discover when and where your anxiety began. You may need to seek professional help with your anxiety.

Inner Child Exercise for Anxiety

Refer back to the inner child exercises. Start with a safe place and relax. Close your eyes and think back to the very first time you remember experiencing anxiety in your life. Document your answers.

When was the first time I remember feeling:

- Anxiety?
- Extreme nervousness?
- Overwhelmed?
- Out of control?
- High levels of stress?

Next questions:

Now that you have pinpointed when you felt anxious, nervous, overwhelmed, etc.

Physically where am I the first time I had this feeling?

What is happing around me?

How old am I?

How do I feel about the situation?

Is there anyone else involved?

What are they doing or saying?

Once you see your anxiety from a different perspective, you might be able to discredit some of your beliefs.

Follow-up questions for your anxiety triggers:

Am I in trouble or danger now? If so, what can I do to change my situation?

Do I have control over my situation?

Am I choosing to be fearful of something from my past? Why?

Is there any valid reason for my feelings at this point in my life?

Am I carrying something from my past that doesn't apply to my current life?

Am I holding on to something that isn't true and doesn't serve me now?

What will it take for me to let go of my past and live in the now?

At one time, I feared everything from what people thought of me to people themselves. I lived in a constant state of fear and anxiety while acting as if everything was all right; I projected an "I can handle everything" persona.

Early on, these were some of the thoughts that consumed my mind: What if I'm not a good enough mother and make the wrong decisions for my children or me? What if I don't have enough money to pay my bills or even to survive?

With all of these thoughts came unhealthy relationships and a life full of anxiety. I constantly questioned my ability to make healthy decisions as I put myself in challenging financial and emotionally hurtful situations. Once I changed my thoughts and my actions, things started to change for the better.

When I would find myself at a crossroads and doubt my ability to make a healthy decision, I would stop and ask myself, "What have I learned from my past? What is best for me now? What can I do about the situation?"

When I would think or say a fearful statement (example: "Omg I can't pay my bills"), I would stop and ask myself: "How can I produce more money so I can pay my bills?" I would follow up by telling myself, "I'm getting better with my finances, and it will all work out for the best." I would focus on what I could do instead of what I couldn't do, which changed my perspective from a panic victim to an optimistic survivor.

Once I started focusing on what I could do, I began to feel better about myself, and I noticed that I wasn't as scared anymore. I learned to trust my decisions, knowing if I didn't like the result of what I had chosen, I could always make a different choice next time. I started believing in myself. Once I focused on having enough money and learned to make better decisions with my money, I had less drama in my life. I also learned to let go of whatever challenges I couldn't change or control. I chose to have faith in myself and something bigger than me.

Belly Breathing Exercise
(Fear, worry, anxiety, and anger)

This is a great exercise to help you relax and self-soothe. The first step to learning how to belly breathe, put your hands on your stomach, near your navel. Take a couple of deep breaths. Do your hands move outward or inward when you inhale? The goal is for your hands to move outward or expand as you inhale; then let your hands move inward as you exhale. This is how babies breathe at birth. The goal is to focus on your breath instead of your anxiety while relaxing.

Breathing Exercise Steps:

1. Inhale deeply and let your stomach expand outward as you fill your diaphragm and lungs with air for the count of four.

2. Exhale deeply and let your stomach collapse and fall inward as you expel all of the air out of your chest, stomach, and diaphragm for the count of four.

3. As you do the exercise, I want you to only focus on your breath while you count. Inhale and exhale each for the count of four, five consecutive times until you feel calm and relaxed. Repeat as necessary.

As you do this exercise, you can expand your inhalations and exhalations longer if you like. The goal is to expel and release your fear, worry, anger, or anxiety as you breathe and count.

Reactions to Fear:

Conquering fear comes when you discover your confidence and courage while having faith in yourself and something bigger. Start facing your fears and learn to analyze your situations. When you are fearful, ask yourself the following questions:

Am I in danger?

How bad is this situation?

What can I do?

What is the worst thing that might happen?

Do I have a valid reason to be fearful in this situation?

Is this an old fear appearing in my current life?

Am I putting myself in dangerous situations? (If so, get help.)

I tell myself on a daily basis, "I am safe, and everything is as it should be." Once you trust in yourself and something bigger, you will always know you are not alone, and everything happens as it is meant to. We just don't always understand why at the time.

Reactions to Worry:

The more you learn to trust in yourself while having faith that things will work out, the more your worry will dissipate. When worry appears, stop and think about the following questions:

Is this thing (person, issue or event) I'm worried about even my concern?

If no, send good thoughts and let it go!

Does this situation pertain directly to my personal life?

If yes, do something and create a solution.

If yes, but you can't control the situation, let it go and give it to something bigger.

Always make sure it's your responsibility to be involved in the first place. If it is, do something about the situation; if not, consider letting something bigger have your worries and let it go.

Reactions to Stress and Anxiety:

Some people carry anxiety from their past for many years. The following step may help you eliminate past anxiety, or you can visit Mannettemorgan.com and get my anxiety audio.

Steps to Dealing with Anxiety

1. Understand where your anxiety originated from so you can start addressing the root cause or even dismiss it, especially if it doesn't apply to your life today.

2. Learn how to manage your anxiety by changing your thoughts from fear-based thoughts to more positive thoughts.

3. Incorporate the anti-anxiety exercises that work best for you and your situation. I personally think the Belly Breathing Exercise and the anxiety audio on my website can help in moments of intense anxiety.

4. Take ownership of what is within your control, and then create a plan to resolve your situation, once you make a decision to take some kind of action, your anxiety levels should improve.

If none of these steps work, you may need to consult a physician or therapist to get help controlling your anxiety – especially if it is limiting you from living a healthy life.

Affirmations for Fear, Worry and Anxiety:

I'm choosing to give my fear to something bigger than me.

I am safe and secure.

I am in the process of learning to let go of my fear or worry.

I only focus on what I can control or do.

I release my worry and know in my heart that everything will work out.

I'm learning to see more positive options in the world.

I find peace and comfort within myself as I face each day.

I know I have the potential to live a healthy, happy, and calm life.

I face my stress with confidence and know this situation will pass.

Anger

Anger: A strong feeling of annoyance, displeasure, or hostility; it is a feeling that is oriented toward some real or supposed grievance.

You are going to experience anger, especially after abuse. Similar to our other emotions, we learn how to deal (or not deal) with our anger from our parents or the people closest to us.

We all get angry; the difference is how we express our anger. We all have a choice to either let anger consume our emotions and behaviors, hold it in or express it in a respectful way. Anger has the ability to eat you up from the inside out.

As a survivor, you can avoid dealing with your anger, or you can find yourself living in a constant state of anger. The real challenge is deciphering if you are experiencing your old anger and your current, authentic anger.

Your current situation may not be the basis of your anger, though it agitates you or reminds you of old anger from your childhood or abuse. Once you can recognize which anger you are experiencing (past or present), you want to find constructive, healthy ways to express it. If your anger has become a dominating, overwhelming constant in your life, you might consider seeking help from a professional or start releasing your anger with some of the exercises throughout this chapter.

Which kind of anger is impacting your life and current relationships? (past or present)

I was a master of holding in my anger. After three years of therapy, I still wouldn't express my anger freely. I continued to hold it in and let it eat away at me from the inside out. I feared that if I let it out, I would lose control. As a child, I learned from my father that anger is always expressed randomly with no rational reasoning at whoever is available and vulnerable. I also learned from my mother that you never express your anger until you can't hold it in anymore. Then you release your anger and frustration all at once toward the person responsible.

I held in every frustration and resentful feeling that I felt for my cousin, my ex-husband, and my father. I let all of those feelings boil and fester inside me for years. In my late twenties, I started dealing with my anger issues. I started addressing my frustration and anger when it happened within a reasonable time by communicating how I felt and what I didn't like. Later, I started releasing my past anger by using the Expel Writing Exercise and approached anger as just another emotion without fear.

 REFLECTIONS

- Why do I get angry?
- What do I get angry about?
- Who do I get angry at?
- When do I express my anger?
- How do I express my anger?
- Do I feel angry more than not in my daily life?

(If so, you may be experiencing past anger that you haven't addressed.)

Recall Exercise

Anger is another emotion you might be able to release by using the inner child exercise. Close your eyes and think back to the very first time you experienced anger. This can be you getting angry or someone close to you getting angry. When, where, or what was the story behind the anger you experienced or witnessed? Write down what you discover.

Let's focus on how others around you express their anger. This can be a parent, friend, family member, or your abuser.

How did they act? Did I even know why they were angry?

Were they in control or out of control?

How did I feel as they became angry?

How old am I?

How did you personally experience anger?

Why am I angry?

What happened?

How old am I?

How did I react?

What did I do or say?

Did I feel in control or out of control?

Was I allowed to express my anger or not?

Was I taught to suppress my anger?

Was I taught how to express my anger in a healthy, respectful way?

These questions can help you understand how you formed your personal relationship with anger.

Follow-up Questions:

How did or does my family deal with anger?

How do I deal with my anger today?

Do I allow myself to get angry?

Am I angry more often than not?

Am I dealing or have I dealt with my past anger?

I feel you need to release your old anger, so you have room to replace it with something better. The key is to let yourself express this emotion, and then let it go.

Anger Exercises
(fear, anxiety, and anger)

Here are a few suggestions on how to physically release your past or perpetual anger. Angry is a verb which involves action, so in order to release your anger, I feel you need to take action physically.

Below are some of the exercises I have found to be helpful. You can also do an activity such as:

- Hit and scream into pillows while letting your anger out.

- Scream and vent in the shower, where you have privacy.

- Write letters to the people you're angry at. Use the Expel Writing Exercise.

- Draw or paint pictures that express your feelings of anger. Use the Art Exercise in the workbook.

- Pull, twist, or rip towels to physically release your anger.

- Destroy items you no longer use or need.

- Play a sport where you hit something (racquetball, tennis, kickboxing, batting cages, etc.)

- Take an exercise class.

- Nerf guns and nerf swords can be useful.

- Any kind of physical exercise can be a great healing and releasing tool.

All of these exercises can be a safe and healthy way to release frustration, resentment, and anger. You may need to use more than one of the exercises several times.

Which exercise are you going to do?

Note: It's important to remember not ever to hurt yourself or others —not physically, emotionally, or mentally. You never want to damage or destroy anything of value. Be safe and responsible as you work through your anger issues. These exercises are for you to use until you deal with your past anger. If you find yourself overwhelmed with anger and can only feel relief when you hit or break something, you might consider professional help.

Once I realized my ex-husband and my best friend were having an affair, I found myself in therapy dealing with my childhood abuse as well as my then-current unhealthy situation. I played racquetball several times a week, mostly with men, because they played much more aggressively. When I played, I would imagine the racquetball was the head of my ex-husband and ex-best friend's head. I would even picture their tiny faces on the ball each time I hit it. I never held back and always hit the ball as hard as I could. This activity totally released a lot of pent-up anger, and I found it to be very therapeutic for me while I healed and moved through my situation.

Day-to-Day Anger

Start facing and addressing your anger as it occurs; don't let it build up inside you. That isn't healthy for yourself or the people you have relationships with. When you find yourself angry, stop, think, and ask yourself the following questions:

Why am I angry?

Am I angry at my current situation or something from my past?

Does the intensity of my anger represent my current situation or not?

Am I dealing with compounded anger that has built up over several experiences?

Once you understand your anger and what it relates to, deal with your current emotions and situation first. Then you can privately deal with any past anger you might be projecting into your current situation.

Handling Current Anger:

1. Why am I angry, and where does my anger come from?

2. Express and communicate my anger in an honest and respectful manner.

3. Let it go once I have expressed it, and move on with my life.

Affirmations for Anger:

I'm learning to express my anger in a healthy way.

I'm becoming more comfortable with my anger.

I'm learning to recognize whether my anger is from my past or current situation, then I deal with it appropriately.

I am in the process of facing my anger while learning how to express it in a healthy way.

I can choose how I want to express my anger.

All of the Happy Busters have to do with past emotions resurfacing in your current life.

- If you are constantly worrying about things you can't control, you will create what you don't want.

- If you are always feeling shame for something from your past, you will re-live that shame repeatedly in your present life.

- If you are always angry with everyone and everything, you will create an environment full of obstacles and resentment.

- If you are always afraid of every opportunity or the unknown, you will avoid letting new opportunities into your life while producing fearful situations.

When any or all of the thoughts above occupy your mind, you will have drama and discontent in your life. When you let go of all those negative emotions, you can create a joyful and happier life for yourself and the people you love.

Follow-up Questions:

What would it take for me to let it go of my shame?

What would it take for me to forgive myself?

How have I let worry consume my life?

How am I going to let go of my anxiety?

How am I going to start self-soothing myself?

How am I going to deal with my anger going forward?

What am I gaining by holding on to my Happy Busters?

What is it going to take for me to live a life free of Happy Busters?

Let Go of Your Story

"Let go of your story so you can let go of your pain."

This is the final and most important part of the healing process. I want you to let go of your story so you can let go of your pain. I can't encourage you enough or stress how important it is to feel. To me, feeling is what makes us human and gives us life. It can be beneficial to acknowledge whatever emotions you experienced after abuse, especially the painful ones.

I don't believe you need to re-live your abusive experiences or even remember every detail. That seems like a cruel and torturous journey that no one needs to experience. The purpose of this exercise is to work through what I call your baggage and grieve. If you still have emotions that cause you pain and discomfort, those are probably your baggage. My belief is that you can only truly heal when you let yourself experience and release those old, lingering, painful emotions.

When you write your story, you can use as much or as little detail as you wish. Sometimes the more emotion and detail, the more effective the exercise. It's all about getting in touch with how you felt during and after your abuse. Here are a few questions to consider before you start:

How did I feel during my abuse?

Did I feel manipulated or tricked?

Did I feel out of control?

Did I feel ashamed and embarrassed?

Did I ever grieve for what was taken from me? (childhood, innocence, virginity, independence, safety, etc.)

Was I scared?

Was I angry?

Was I confused?

Was I numb, or did I feel emotionally detached?

Did I want to run, hide, or disappear?

Did I want to hurt my abuser?

Did I want to hurt myself? Have I hurt myself?

Did I finally give up or lose hope?

The objective is to grieve and release all of the emotions you have carried throughout your life. I want you to expel every thought, feeling, and memory onto paper, so you can let your past go once and for all. The goal is to empty your pain and grief so you can replace them with healthy emotions. This exercise can be used multiple times for different situations throughout your life. It can be used for divorce, abuse, past unresolved relationships, and the death of a loved one.

Letting Go of Your Story Writing Exercise
(abuse, divorce, tragedy, or loss of a loved one)

You will need five things to do this exercise: Paper, pen, a small bowl, a safe place to burn and dispose of your paper, and something to comfort you after the exercise.

Set aside one to three hours of personal time to do this exercise. It is important to do this particular exercise by yourself in a private place without children, friends, significant others, or roommates. This exercise is going to be emotional and freeing at the same time. You may even need to take breaks while you write. It will take whatever time is required to work through the process. I want you to prepare yourself for the worst ugly cry ever. If you're like me, that means you might not look so great the next morning, so keep that in mind. I also want you to have some kind of comfort item or activity for after the experience. When I refer to this, I'm referring to ice cream, tea, chocolate, favorite blanket, your favorite movie to watch afterward or a relaxing bath. Make sure you have whatever it is you need to comfort and console yourself when you're finished. You may want to consider doing something special for yourself the next day (massage, pedicure, dinner out, hike with a supportive person, etc.)

Create a safe and comfortable space to do this exercise. You may want candles or music. As you write, don't worry about grammar, spelling or legibility; just get the story out and on the page.

1. Take a few deep breaths before you start, then tell yourself how much you love yourself for doing this.

2. **Start writing your story.** You can write as much or as little detail as you want, but remember the more emotion expressed, the more healing that will take place. Refer to the questions above if you have trouble getting started. Then write until every feeling and emotion has been expressed onto the pages. (When I did this, my tears covered the pages as much as my words. That's expected! Let everything fall away as you release your story.) Grieve for what you have lost and for the pain you encountered. Take a break if you need one, but continue until every word, tear and emotion are on that paper.

3. When you're done, sit for a moment and **just breathe.** Give yourself a huge hug and congratulate yourself on an emotional task well done. You have shown amazing courage and determination to complete this exercise. It is time to get that ice cream, movie, or whatever comforts you.

4. Take your pages and crumple them up or tear them up and **put them into the bowl.** You don't need to read the pages, but if you feel a strong desire to read them, by all means, do so one last time. You experienced it, you've written it, you've cried, and now it's time to let it go.

5. You are going to conduct your **letting go ceremony** with fire. It's time to liberate yourself from your pain and your past. Make this your celebration of closure and freedom. I want you to burn your pages in a pot, fireplace, or fire pit. Watch them dissolve into ashes, knowing that part of your life is over. You don't need to re-live it again. You can do this alone or with a loving, trusting, supportive friend, or partner; it is your choice.

6. It's time to let go of your story and your past once and for all. You are the only one that can heal your heart. Remember the past is the past, and you are learning to live for today.

7. You may need to take some time for yourself and maybe even mourn for your past and what you lost. Let it all go and give yourself grace so you can continue to heal. When you're done mourning, stand up, put your shoulders back, and start being the healthy survivor you were always meant to be.

How do you feel? I personal felt emotionally drained but also lighter, freer, and stronger. I actually felt my heart sigh with relief and renewed hope. I am so proud of you for taking on this exercise. I realize it can be overwhelming.

Follow-up Questions:

Once you have calmed down, comforted yourself, and had time to reflect on your experience, answer the questions below.

How much more free do I feel after this exercise?

1   2   3   4   5   6   7   8   9   10

How much lighter do I feel after this exercise?

1   2   3   4   5   6   7   8   9   10

How much stronger do I feel after this exercise?

1   2   3   4   5   6   7   8   9   10

How much more at peace do I feel after this exercise?

1   2   3   4   5   6   7   8   9   10

I recognize that this was another heavy chapter, and I commend you for being brave enough to do the work. Look at how far you've come since we began. I'm sure this hasn't been easy. New ways of thinking, along with change, can feel challenging or even impossible. Hopefully, you understand yourself better than before as you tame the Happy Busters, let go of your past and forgive yourself. On the other side of all this work, a healthy, happy, and joyful life awaits you!

Look at how much your tree has grown since you started this book. Simply reading and thinking about where you are as well as how you got here has likely produced new thoughts and even new behaviors. Hopefully, those thoughts have produced strong roots, and your new behaviors have strengthened your trunk. As you have discovered more about yourself, I'm sure the branches of your tree are reaching out for new desires and a blue sky. As you have learned how to forgive yourself and let go of your past, I suspect that now you have all you need to let your tree blossom as you discover more joy and happiness. My wish is that your tree has grown into a magnificent representation of the person inside of you just waiting to be seen.

One-Month Follow-Up Questions

Reflect on the follow-up questions below once a month over the next three months.

How much better do I feel after addressing my shame and guilt?

1   2   3   4   5   6   7   8   9   10

How much better do I feel after addressing my fears?

1   2   3   4   5   6   7   8   9   10

How much better do I feel after addressing my stress and anxiety?

1   2   3   4   5   6   7   8   9   10

How much better do I feel after addressing my anger?

1   2   3   4   5   6   7   8   9   10

How much better do I feel after letting go of my story?

1   2   3   4   5   6   7   8   9   10

How much happier do I feel after applying the Happiness Boosters?

1   2   3   4   5   6   7   8   9   10

CHAPTER 8

Your Relationships with Others

• •

RELATIONSHIPS. WELL, WHAT CAN I SAY? I have acquired an abundance of knowledge in the past 52 years. I have been in relationships that were abusive, challenging, destructive, conditional, and disrespectful; I have also had relationships that were caring, compassionate, trusting, and loving.

My childhood relationships were mostly inconsistent, uncertain, and scary, to say the least. I was a sensitive, creative, outgoing child before I learned it wasn't safe to be. I was fortunate to have a loving mother who accepted and loved me.

My first husband eagerly fulfilled the role of abuser. My marriage was comprised of emotional abuse, conditional love, and disrespect. Unfortunately, I had no self-confidence, self-respect, or boundaries. Throughout this relationship, I learned what wasn't good for me as well as what I didn't want.

261

I entered my second marriage as a survivor, learning about myself and what a healthy relationship can be like. This relationship was based on unconditional love, respect, and trust. During this time, I became comfortable with what I considered a normal, healthy relationship until he, unfortunately, passed away.

I approached my third marriage as an independent, confident woman who understood what I needed, unwilling to settle for less. This relationship has healthy boundaries, unconditional acceptance, love, trust, and mutual respect. We have our struggles just like any other healthy relationship. For example, we found that we communicate very differently. But we respect each other enough that we work through our communication challenges. Today I am living a healthier, happier life with my husband, children, friends, and family.

Now you have nurtured your tree and are growing and expanding all the way from your roots to the tips of each branch as your leaves gleam in the sunshine. Are you aware that an aspen grove's roots are all connected? They may appear to be separate trees above the ground; yet, underneath the soil and rocks, they are actually one organism. This isn't any different for you. Like it or not, you are connected to family, friends, partners, children, coworkers, and even acquaintances. The only difference in your connections is the degree of separation between each person. We are all connected, similar to an aspen grove.

Now that you understand your relationship with yourself, let's focus on your relationships with others. None of us exist alone in this world – even if we feel alone. All of us have had good and not-so-good relationships. As humans, we are social, so we need to interact with other humans. Sadly, surviving abuse has likely affected your relationships with others, even if you're not aware of it. With each relationship, there's a responsibility to yourself and the other person. Now it's time to develop those relationships you have with your partner, children, family, and friends.

> **Healthy Relationships**: Relationships that create physical, mental, or emotional well-being between two people through interaction and connection.
>
> **Trust**: Assured reliance on the character, ability, strength, or truth of someone or something; one in which confidence and faith are placed.

"Let the people you love be the people they want to be."

The Roots of Your Relationships

First and foremost, your relationships need to be safe and free of abuse for you and your children. The following qualities are what I feel are the most vital parts of any relationship:

- Acceptance, Love, Respect, and Trust
- Communication
- Healthy Boundaries

Let's start with The Big 3: unconditional acceptance, love, and self-respect. These qualities should be the mutual foundation of all your relationships, just like they are the foundation of the relationship you have with yourself. I'm going to add trust to your foundation with others, so your relationships are strong as well as secure.

Do you have limits or conditions for the people you love?

When have others placed conditions on their love for you?

Do you judge others for their appearance, size, behaviors, and beliefs?

Do you choose to focus on other's unique qualities and abilities?

When have others recognized your qualities and abilities?

Do you trust the people you're in a relationship with?

Are you trustworthy?

Start discovering more tolerance for others in your life, community, and the world. Tolerance is a willingness to accept beliefs, practices, and behaviors different from our own. We are all part of a community, and that community is connected. Like I said in the beginning, we all learn how to perceive our beliefs and behaviors from our childhood and the community we grew up in. Different cultures practice different religions, beliefs, and customs. Unfortunately, space and distance separate our cultures in our own country and around the world. This can cause us to become defensive and feel separate from others. This separation causes fear and produces intolerance among us as a human race. Once we choose to see each other as similar, while accepting we all believe and behave differently, then we as a human race can show more tolerance and acceptance for our fellow men and women alike. I truly feel healthy relationships involve tolerance, compassion, and a certain amount of empathy. We could all work at being a little more accepting and tolerant of others.

Trust and respect are just as important as tolerance. To trust someone is to have faith and confidence in their character. In fact, if you don't have trust and respect, you will experience turmoil, animosity, and friction.

Along with trust and respect, always leave room for a little humor. Humor makes life bearable. Laughter is essential in hard times and also possesses mental and physical healing properties. It is important to have fun and laughter in any relationship.

The Value of Communication

If you think about it, communication is a vital part of interacting with others. We have the ability to communicate through vocal expression or through our body language. Both can effectively communicate how we feel and sometimes even what we need or want.

Are you comfortable using your voice to express yourself?

When have you expressed how you feel or what you think freely?

As a child, when were you allowed to speak openly?

As a child, was it implied that you should be seen and not heard?

Were you silenced by your abuser?

Are you comfortable being honest with others?

When have you treated others respectfully?

When have you listened and talked equally when having a conversation?

When have you told others what they should or shouldn't do?

When have you assumed you know what other people are going to say before they express themselves?

When have you lied or hid things in your relationships?

We each have a voice, and it's time to work on expressing your voice assertively and authentically. If your voice was suppressed by an abusive relationship, or from growing up in a home where children (or women) were told to be seen and not heard, you might have internalized the lie that your thoughts and beliefs weren't important enough to be heard. This kind of maltreatment could have taught you that your thoughts and beliefs were not important. It's time to express how you feel and what you think.

Honesty: The quality of being fair and truthful with integrity; free from harshness.

Passive-aggressive behavior: Indirect expression of hostility. It is manipulative behavior, without being open or direct, while being forceful or exhibiting aggression. This behavior will usually leave you feeling dissatisfied, frustrated, or disrespected, but powerless to resolve it effectively.

Narcissist: A person that is extremely self-centered with an exaggerated sense of self-importance; they are marked by characteristics of excessive admiration or infatuation with oneself.

Communication Rules

I feel these are excellent rules for communications. Write down these communication rules or take the cards from your *Finding Your Voice* workbook. Then put them on your bulletin board or refrigerator, where everyone in your home can see them. Your goal is to use these rules with your children, partner, and other relationships.

See, Hear, and Listen

Practice Calm, Direct, and Respectful Communication

Communicate Honestly and Truthfully

Ask *Could You* instead of asserting *You Should*

Express How You Feel

Never Assume

Get on The Same Page

See, Hear and Listen

We all want to be seen and heard while being treated with respect. Everyone wants to express their thoughts, ideas, and opinions while feeling heard. Learning to really listen without judgment while engaging in conversations with others is one of the most respectful things to offer in any of your relationships.

The goal is to listen to others before you respond. Slow down, take a deep breath, and think about what you want to say before responding - especially in heated conversations or differences of opinions. You can save yourself a lot of heartaches when you contemplate responses before you open your mouth. You truly can't take back what you say once it's said.

Note: If you feel you have a relationship with someone who is insensitive, dominating, or overly self-important, you could be dealing with someone who is narcissistic. Having a relationship with someone who has narcissistic tendencies isn't healthy for anyone. You may want to evaluate your relationship if you find yourself feeling unappreciated and unworthy of being an equal partner.

Practice Calm, Direct and Respectful Communication

Learn to communicate calmly and respectfully with everyone, even if they aren't calm and respectful. The calmer you are, the less defensive others will be. Your goal in any relationship is to mutually support one another while maintaining a certain amount of individually.

Keep your conversations respectful and direct. Don't use passive-aggressive tactics to get your way. Do you know someone that guilts others into doing what they want or exhibits forceful indirect behavior to get their way? If so, this is passive-aggressive behavior; it is an unhealthy type of communication, especially for someone who has been abused trying to reclaim their self-respect.

When my daughter was a teenager, I recall her friends screaming and fighting with their mothers. It broke my heart to see them treat each other with such disrespect. We forget that once someone starts screaming, no one is listening. My mom always said treat others the way you want to be treated, and then you never have to say you're sorry; this especially applies to your children. I always treated my children with the utmost respect, even when I didn't agree with them. I taught them to express themselves in a calm, respectful way so we could take turns communicating our feelings. We didn't always agree on certain situations, but we always maintained a respectful dialogue with acceptance and a certain amount of compromise.

In my view, communication shouldn't be disrespectful or involve screaming. Raising your voices shows a lack of respect between both people. When we learn to express ourselves calmly while communicating our needs, wants, and feelings, it's easier to maintain respectful, healthy relationships.

Communicate Honestly and Truthfully

Remember to be respectful, honest, and truthful in all of your conversations. That doesn't mean you can't be gentle and compassionate at the same time. Honesty is the quality of being truthful with integrity. I have a friend who says, "Don't go along in order to get along." In other words, don't say or do things you don't want to just for the sake of being compliant. It's important to do things for other people, but you don't have to sacrifice yourself or your needs in the process. Every relationship is a give-and-take partnership.

Note: Only ask questions you are willing to hear a truthful answer to. Don't set yourself up for disappointment unless you are willing to take responsibility for an answer you may not like. When someone asks me difficult questions, I have been known to preface my answers by responding, "Do you really want to hear my honest opinion?" It's better to give someone an option before telling them something they don't want to hear.

Ask Could You Instead of Insisting You Should

Start asking *could you* and stop demanding what you think others should do. Do you like it when someone tells you what to do? I think we all would rather be asked than told. People tend to be defensive when ordered around. When you ask *could you* the other person has a choice. Who wouldn't want a choice?

Example: Consider the difference when you take demands out of your conversations: "You should help me clean the house." becomes the nicer, "Could you help me clean the house?"

Express How You Feel

It's best to let someone know how you feel instead of holding others responsible for how they make you feel. The truth is you choose how you feel about everything. No one person can make you feel any certain way. You have to choose to participate in your feelings and reactions. Saying, "You make me feel a certain way" creates a defensive connotation similar to using *you should*. This can also apply to your positive emotions "I only feel happy when I'm with you." You ultimately don't want to relinquish your emotions to others. Your feelings are fully yours to experience and express – positive or negative.

Example: Consider the difference: "I feel great when I am with you," instead of, "You make me feel great when I'm with you." by keeping your comments centered around your emotions you empower yourself to own what you're feeling, rather than putting the power of making you feel good in someone else's hands. The same goes in owning difficult conversations. For example, "I sometimes don't feel heard when we are talking," instead of "You don't listen to me when I'm talking to you!" You are taking ownership and responsibility of your feelings rather than throwing the blame onto someone else and setting them up to be defensive.

Never Assume

Never assume you know what someone else is thinking or wanting. Assuming is just a way of making an ass of yourself. Listen to what others are saying while keeping an open mind. Don't get stuck in a response you desire to hear. Refrain from becoming defensive or shifting the conversation to your own opinion.

REFLECTIONS

- Do you really know what others need or want?

- Can you see someone else's experience through their eyes?

- Can you truly feel what they feel?

None of us truly understand how someone else sees their own experiences or the world. Perception is in the eye of the beholder, similar to how beauty is in the eye of the beholder. Two people may experience a similar type of abuse, but their perception is never the same. We all see, hear, and feel our emotions with different reactions and intensity. What might be humiliating to one person may be traumatizing to another. Each person experiences life through different-colored glasses. Some of us see the world through rose-colored glasses while others of us only see a dark, gray haze that obstructs our view.

So, it's best never to assume you understand how someone else perceives their life experiences. The goal is to learn how to respect and empathize with others. This does not mean you need to take on their challenges or emotional pain. The conclusion is never either presume or assume you know how someone feels or what they need; you will only end up pushing the other person away while making an ass of yourself.

Same Page

Good communication comes with a clear understanding of what the other person is saying. Once a person has expressed a thought, need, or desire always ask for clarification by repeating it back. Reflect what you think you heard in the form of a question. Next, ask them if you are correct or not. If not, try again until you are on the same page and understand what each other is trying to communicate. Always remain patient and respectful, listening to one another throughout the process.

Example: If your partner says, "I feel like you don't trust me with our money because you are always questioning what I buy." You say, "Are you saying, you feel I'm always questioning how you spend our money, and this is causing trust issues between us?" If they say yes you are done, if not, keep communicating until you both understand and are on the same page.

My husband and I struggle to this day when it comes to communicating with each other. The truth is we speak different languages even though we both speak English. He is an engineer and is precise and direct. I'm a little more creative and touchy-feely when expressing myself. I use adjectives and generalities, which just confuse him. He is looking for direct questions and answers with precise detail. We often find ourselves having to ask each other what the other person is trying to say quite frequently. Eventually, we get on the same page, after a few rounds explaining ourselves.

We also struggle with assuming we know what the other person needs, wants, or is referring to. So, we both continue to make asses of ourselves over and over again. I think it is because we have been together for so long. Along with comfortable companionship comes a presumption, you know someone better than you do.

Three Basic Steps of Communication

Write down the list below or go to your *Finding Your Voice* workbook and remove the Communication Cards. Keep these cards close, use them daily, until you know them by heart.

1. Stop, be present, listen.

2. Think before you respond. Never react without thinking. Remember, you have the ability to hurt others with your words. Some people say you should say whatever you think. Do you really want to hear every thought someone else has toward you or all of their opinions? Probably not. Show others the same consideration and respect by evaluating your responses before you speak.

3. Finally, respond with tolerance, compassion, and gentle honesty.

Communicating and Connecting with Body Language

We also communicate through our body language. Your body language and what you are verbally communicating needs always to be congruent. If you are saying one thing and your body is defensive, others will recognize your body language even if they aren't aware of it. The following are some different types of body languages you may want to become aware of so you can maintain a respectful relationship:

- Eye contact is everything. It says you are listening, you're interested, and most of all, you respect the person you are communicating with. Learn to keep your body language engaged as you communicate. Stay focused on the person you are having a conversation with and don't let distractions divert your attention.

- Try not to cross your arms while listening or talking to someone, especially while nodding your head, yes. When you do this, you are sending two different messages. Nodding yes says you agree while crossing your arms says you are defensive and may disagree. You wouldn't shake your head no while agreeing with someone, would you?

- Don't point your finger at someone. It is just another form of intimidation or bullying. Don't roll your eyes either; it says you think the other person is stupid, unimportant, or unworthy of your respect.

- Get on the same physical level, especially with children. Sit next to them or squat down in front of a child. Eye-level is best. Try not to stand or sit behind a desk when you are having a serious conversation with someone close to you. This behavior can display dominance. It's important to be physically open and compassionate when communicating with people close to you.

Healthy Boundaries

Certain relationships, especially the ones you have with a partner or spouse, need to be based on a certain amount of equal interest, goals, principles, and values. You also want to be equally committed and find some commonality in how you see the world. Share an intention to grow together and not apart. The goal is to be independent people working together as a unified pair. In the words of Thomas A. Harris, *"I'm okay, you're okay, and together we can be great."*

Start trusting yourself and your abilities while setting better boundaries in all of your relationships. You are no longer a victim waiting to be taken advantage of. You are a strong individual, learning to live a healthier life with better boundaries. Embrace who you are, including the great qualities you bring to your relationships. Write down the items below or take the Healthy Boundaries cards from your *Finding Your Voice* workbook. This is what I consider to be healthy boundaries:

Embrace the Words *Yes* and *No*

Compromise

Set Guidelines in Your Relationships

Master Your Reactions

Don't Try to Change or Control Others

Don't Try to Fix Others, Fix Yourself

Embrace the Words *Yes* and *No*

Learn to balance your yes's, and no's in every one of your relationships. Say *yes* to living a happier and healthier life, while saying *no* to what you don't want and what isn't healthy for you. *Yes* can be a great word for those who are more introverted and shy, yes is a way to incorporate more interaction and activities into your life. *No* is a powerful word because it lets you express individual independence, especially when you don't attach any guilt to it.

When I was younger, I would constantly let others take advantage of me. I would help anyone and everyone instead of taking care of my own responsibilities and myself. I would struggle to tell someone *no* when they would ask me for help, even if I didn't really want to. If I choose to say no, I would lie and make excuses while experiencing a tremendous amount of guilt. After some time in therapy, I started using the word no more regularly and even learned not to make excuses. Now I'm more comfortable with the word no when I don't want to do something, I just politely say no and proceed with my life.

Parenting Note: Parents, it is important to use both *yes* and *no* equally when it comes to your children. Both words can be the building block for a respectful, trusting relationship. There is nothing wrong with telling your children no. You have limits on what you do; they should too!

Compromise

Compromise means to come to an agreement by mutual concession. As a survivor, you don't want to let another dominate you; there is always room for compromise in every relationship. Healthy relationships seek out mutually-agreeable resolutions to conflict through negotiation. Both parties need to be willing to find solutions within their challenges. If you have a tendency to give too much, or let others take advantage of you, start standing up for yourself and take better care of your own needs and wants. Stop, think, and ask yourself,

"Does the resolution to the situation benefit both of us?" A compromise to any conflict needs to be mutually beneficial.

Set Guidelines in Your Relationships

Share all responsibilities with your partner. These can include parenting decisions, family decisions, equally-distributed household chores, financial decisions, and consenting sexual acts. All decisions should be beneficial to all parties. Discern behaviors in your relationships that are unhealthy for you and them so you can make the necessary changes.

REFLECTIONS

- What are my expectations in this relationship (with family obligations, parenting, finances, etc.)?
- What do I need and want out of this relationship (as a wife, mother, business partner, etc.)?
- What are acceptable, healthy behaviors for me in my relationships? (respect, compassion, honesty, love, trust, etc.)
- Does anything in this relationship remind me of an unhealthy past relationship?
- If so, what?
- How can I change it?

Parenting Notes: Parents, by setting boundaries and guidelines you are teaching your children to respect you, others, and society.

You also may want to share household responsibilities along with limited family decisions. Everyone is equally important and has a responsibility to the family unit.

Master of Your Reactions

Sometimes it feels like we don't have control of our reactions, but we do. We have control of our thoughts, which create our actions and reactions. Use your thoughts and emotions together and learn to react confidently and respectfully. Have you ever said or did something you wish you hadn't? Like I said earlier, words and actions can be hurtful, and you truly can't take back what you said or did; apologizing can't really change what's done. Avoid saying or doing something you will regret.

As a survivor, some of your emotions can be intensified, so double-check and make sure you are dealing with current emotions, not past feelings. If you find yourself dealing with past emotions, you may need to go back and do some more self-work in chapters four or seven. If you struggle with overreacting, ask yourself the following questions:

REFLECTIONS

- Is this reaction pertaining to a current situation, or is it something from my past?

- If I overreact to this situation, is it going to help the outcome of the situation?

- If I overreact to this situation, will this create drama I don't want or need?

- How important is this situation to me?

- Do I really know all the facts, or am I assuming I know?

Parenting Note: If you are an emotionally intense parent, remember that your children are affected by your behaviors. They deserve your unconditional acceptance, love, and most of all, respect. You want to respect your children enough that you treat them with the same dignity you would give an adult. We always want to support our children with healthy emotional and physical growth.

Don't Try to Change or Control Others

People are who they are – nothing more, nothing less. People can choose to change, but no matter how much you love them, you will never force them to change. Each individual has their own expectations of who and what they want to be. Remember, no one made you go on your journey of healing; you chose this path. I'm not saying that you should accept abusive behaviors. Those kinds of behaviors have no place in your life today. I'm saying that if someone is mostly healthy, acceptance of their limitations and flaws is necessary.

Parenting Note: Parents, your job is to guide and lead your children. Do not try to control them. They will only rebel. Demonstrate and lead your children by example. Teach them how to make healthy decisions and live healthy lives. They will respect you more for walking the walk and living by what you teach. Children learn by watching and emulating what they see and hear. Remember to accept, love and respect them unconditionally.

Don't Try to Fix Others, Fix Yourself

Live your life and let the people you care about live theirs; this includes your partner, family, friends, coworkers, and grown children. Your responsibility is to take care of yourself and your children until they are grown. You can choose to be compassionate and supportive, but it isn't your job to be a codependent, enabler, therapist, or caretaker for everyone or their issues. Each individual has a responsibility to take care of themselves. We, as survivors tend to take on other people's issues and even their emotions. We sometimes try to fix the world instead of ourselves.

Start living an independent life. You do not need the drama of friends and family because more than likely you have enough of your own. If you are the type of person that gets involved in other people's situations and is immersed in other's lives, ask yourself the following questions:

 REFLECTIONS

- How is this any of my business?

- How does this involve me, my children, or partner?

- Why do I need to be involved in this situation? (Maybe not?)

- Why do I need to know more information about this situation? (Maybe not?)

Example: If your sister calls and shares her personal challenge, you can listen and even offer advice if she asks for it! But once you hang up the phone, you need to let her issues go. You don't need to take on her problems and make them your own.

Sometimes we are just present when other people's shit starts flying. We need to learn to recognize it for what it is and maybe even be compassionate, then get out of the way and let them deal with it.

Follow-up Questions:

What would it take for you to set better boundaries in your relationships?

What would it take for you to learn to say *no*?

How do you maintain a healthy give-and-take in your relationships?

When you compromise, does it benefit both parties?

Do you still let people take advantage of you? Who?

Are you an equal partner in your relationships?

Are you co-dependent or an enabler to the people you have relationships with?

When do you choose to emotionally take on other people's issues, challenges, or emotions?

What would it take for you to stop and think before you react to situations in your relationships?

Do you try to control people? Who?

Do you let others live their lives their way? Who?

Care Enough to Understand Those Close to You

A vital part of any relationship is taking time to understand the individual personality of the person you have a relationship with. They more than likely don't think, process, behave, or believe, exactly as you do. Guess what? Just because we have the same DNA or we are partners with someone doesn't mean we perceive life in the same way.

This is why I feel it is important to take time to learn more about the people you are choosing to spend your life with. No one can read your mind, and you can't read theirs. *The 5 Love Languages* by Gary Chapman can help you learn how to meet each other's emotional needs in order to feel loved. The knowledge you can gain from this book can improve and strengthen your relationships. I highly recommend you read this book and share it with others. To take the test, go to http://www.5lovelanguages.com/profile/

The following are the 5 types of Love Languages:

Words of Affirmation

Acts of Service

Receiving gifts

Quality Time

Physical Touch

283

Love Language Exercise

Once each family member learns their individual love languages, I want you to start incorporating them into your daily life. Take your *Finding Your Voice* workbook and list each family member's top two love languages, if two and three are equal include both as you proceed. Prepare a notecard for each family member, then place the card on the refrigerator or bulletin board to remind everyone of each other's love languages. The following exercise can help your family unit become more connected while feeling more loved. Each member of the family is to do the following steps daily.

1. Once a day, give each family member one of their love languages and keep giving it for three weeks.

2. When you receive love based on your love language from another family member acknowledge and recognize them for their contribution, especially during the first few weeks.

When everyone participates by doing the exercise along with the other activities from this chapter, it is amazing how everyone in the family unit will be happier and feel more loved.

The Differences Between Men and Women

It's important to consider the differences between men and women. We are physically and emotionally different. It's vital that we recognize how differently we process our thoughts and emotions. We as women, have to quit expecting men to think and feel the way we do. Ladies, they just aren't made like us.

If you were abused by a male, you likely learned to be submissive, even made to feel secondary to men in general or you could still possess an overwhelming fear of them. We are all human, though we may not process emotions and thoughts in the same way. Example: Most females are taught from a young age to be nurturing. This quality can lead to nagging and worrying behaviors that we can carry throughout our lives. On the other hand, being nurturing may not be emphasized in a young man's life.

Insight into Men

Men tend to focus on solutions and conclusions. Men usually focus on practical issues and how those issues affect a situation. They want to fix issues and move on to the next thing. They can be true problem solvers. When it comes to men, don't ask if you don't want a solution. (Keep in mind, when communicating with men sometimes it's best to let them know you do not want a solution you just want them to listen.) It goes the same way when asking a man what they think of your outfit. To them, this is a trick question. Most of them have learned to respond in a positive way, but their natural instinct is to tell you truthfully what they think. If they tell you the truth, have no taste in clothes, and don't appreciate your style, this can end with a less-than-positive reaction. Men are more direct, and their directness can be abrasive. This goes back to when I said, don't ask if you don't want their true opinion.

If you find yourself trying to communicate with them and feel the conversation is usually one-sided on your part, then stop talking and give them time to express themselves while they gather their thoughts. You may want to take time to listen without assuming you know what they are going to say. Some men really struggle to communicate with the opposite sex and even find us perplexing. Most men really don't understand women in general. Try not to take their confusion and directness personally. Have you ever met a man that didn't find farts funny? Probably not. Most of them just aren't made like us.

Usually, when men are quiet, it does not mean anything. (This does not apply to all men or every situation.) But in general, men do not consume their minds with the same things women do. When men are focused and quiet, they are probably just thinking about work, sports, a hobby, etc. Don't try to read anything into it. Let them be. Their thoughts are typically not totally focused on you or your friend's issues.

Insight into Women

Women are more vocal about everything, and women gather and share all kinds of information. Women tend to be focused on emotional issues and how those issues can affect themselves and others.

Women appreciate being heard. Why do you think you love your girlfriends? Girlfriends listen. It isn't always necessary for someone to fix your issues, but instead empathize with you as they listen to your situation. Women bounce ideas out into the world so they can solve big and small world issues.

Women, as a whole, especially if they have survived abuse, tend to read more into situations or make things more profound than they actually are. Female abuse survivors may overanalyze experiences because of oversensitivity. If you find yourself oversensitive or overanalyzing situations, step back and ask yourself these questions from chapter four and seven: Is it true? Is it any of my business? Is it as bad as I think?

As women, it would be great if we could all learn not to sweat the small stuff and only take on the issues we are responsible for. You have to choose to let go of what you can't control and react to what you can.

Finally, I feel it's a gift to teach our girls and boys that strength is just as much a female quality as a masculine one. Be a strong woman who wants to debate the hard issues and change the world for the better so your daughters will be confident, strong and self-reliant, and your sons will respect confident, strong, independent women.

Understanding Your Past Relationships

Our past relationships can hold the answer to what we need and want as well as what we don't want in our current relationships. Really look at the people you have chosen to associate with throughout your life. If you want to have healthy relationships going forward, learn how to recognize red flags and unhealthy behaviors from your past and present relationships.

Which of your relationships was challenging, abusive, unhealthy, manipulative, controlling, or full of drama? This can include romantic relationships, family relationships, as well as friendships you had or still have. Learn to discern personality traits and destructive behaviors. Reflect on how past partners reacted and behaved in different situations. Also, pay close attention to how you reacted to their behaviors.

Learn from Your Past

Take your *Finding Your Voice* workbook and make a list of every relationship you have had that has been challenging, abusive, unhealthy, manipulative, controlling, or full of drama. Once you have assembled your list, answer the questions below, and observe what you did and didn't like in each relationship.

REFLECTIONS

- Were they kind and compassionate?

- How would I honestly describe this person to someone else?

- How did they treat me, others, children, or animals?

- Which of their behaviors and actions caused me pain and drama?

- How intense were their emotions?

- Did they have any anger issues?

- Did they overreact to certain situations?

- Did they use passive-aggressive behaviors to get what they wanted? How?

- Were they manipulative? How?

- Were they controlling? How?

- Were they narcissistic? How?

- Was I afraid of them? Why?

- What other kinds of drama or chaos did I experience while I was with them?

- How was my relationship unhealthy?

- Was there anything about them I liked or loved? What?

- What behaviors did I like?

- Why did I love them?

- Why did I remain in a relationship with them?

Note: Most of your answers above indicate red flags. These are great warning signs for you to pay attention to going forward.

Red Flags

It's imperative that you learn to trust yourself and your ability to recognize red flags and warning signs. Trusting in our decision-making abilities is something we all strive for after surviving abuse. Our ultimate goal is to do what is right for ourselves and our children. Do any of these sound like something you might say?

"I am never having another relationship because my relationships always fail."

"Why do I always pick people that have as much or more drama than me?"

"Why do I always pick the wrong one, bad one, or the person that hurts me?"

It's possible you don't trust yourself or your ability to choose a partner or friends. You have to learn how to trust yourself and your ability to discern healthy people from unhealthy people. You possess the ability to make better choices for yourself. Take everything you have learned in this book and start choosing people that come from a healthy background or who have overcome their own unhealthy experiences. Trust your intuition as well as your logic and listen to your authentic self that knows when to stay and when to run. Here are a few questions that can help you examine if you want to consider pursuing a new relationship:

REFLECTIONS

- Why do I want to pursue this relationship?

- What does this person have to offer me?

- Do this person's behaviors appear to be healthy?

- Does this person seem to be open, honest, and trustworthy?

- Does this person seem to be caring, kind, and considerate?

- Does this person have a healthy relationship with their family, children or ex, if divorced? If not, why?

- Does this person seem to have his or her shit together? Or not?

- Would I think this person was good for my best friend, sister or daughter?

Learn to become someone who pays attention to other people's behaviors. I feel how we all behave is a reflection of who we are. Our behavior gives some insight into our personal emotional health and well-being. If the person you are considering having a relationship with doesn't meet your qualifications, why would you disrespect yourself by moving forward with the relationship? Is this the best person for you and your life, going forward? Why would you consider an unhealthy relationship after all you have learned?

It's time to take responsibility for your life and learn to recognize unhealthy behaviors, so you don't continue in unhealthy relationships going forward. They say the definition of insanity is trying the same thing over and over again while expecting a different result. Why not try something or (someone) different? You just might get a different result. By doing so, you are learning to break the cycle of abuse while choosing to survive in this world.

Learning from Your Experiences

If you have had challenging relationships, at least learn from them. Like I said, our past is the secret to our future. You can always figure out new ways to react to different personalities, behaviors, and situations. Start by replaying a situation several times in your mind with different outcomes. Think about how you could have put forth more patience, tolerance, assertiveness, or simply a different reaction that was better for you or the situation. Replay it with different scenarios so you can master which way you want to behave or act in a similar future situation. As you replay your situation, ask yourself the following questions:

🌿 REFLECTIONS

- Could I have handled my situation better? How?

- Could I have applied a different behavior or reaction? What?

- Could I have had more tolerance or patience in this situation? How?

- Could I have stood up for myself more? How?

- Could I have done something differently? What?

- Could a new reaction benefit me and/or the other people involved? What reaction?

- How do I want to handle this situation if it arises again?

Relationship Obstacles

When we change, it forces change in most of our relationships, like it or not. As a result of your changes, some people close to you will adapt and even make changes of their own; others will not. You may even desire for certain individuals around you to change, but that isn't your decision. I have tried to encourage and change others I care about, but my efforts were futile. They are on their own journey, which may not include the change you desire for them.

You may even choose to give up certain relationships. Some of the people you have relationships with will struggle with your independence and may never accept the new, independent you.

Realistically, you may find some of these people slowly exiting your life. Don't be alarmed. People come and go, especially as we change and heal.

I feel we have periods of growth with big steps forward then a few backward. In the beginning, you may revert back to your teenage attitude and think you know everything, or you may start over-compensating in certain areas of your life. You may become more abrupt while setting hard boundaries. You may become more defiant with others or feel the need to prove your opinions or beliefs as you stand up for yourself. This is the time when most survivors find themselves disagreeing or arguing in order to secure their place as an independent person, even if they have been submissive their entire lives.

Keep in mind what we learn and overcome is usually what we teach, preach and express to others. As you continue to heal, you will realize how unimportant some issues truly are, and then you will surrender your need to be right and let others have their own opinions and beliefs without judgment. The following is a little insight for you to consider:

- What people think about you is actually what they are judging in themselves.
- When you take things personally, it's likely your own self-criticism, not theirs. Unless they are overly insecure.
- Not everything is about you.
- Needing to be right implies everyone else is wrong.

A few years ago, I was driving when the person in front of me suddenly slammed on their brakes. To me, they seemed to be stopping for no apparent reason, so I beeped my horn. They proceeded to give me the bird. As I looked in the rearview mirror, I realized there was an ambulance coming in the distance. I had my music playing so loudly, I didn't hear it coming.

Here are examples of how we can change our perception as we grow and heal.

The young Mannette, who was afraid and fearful, would have put her head down, feeling awful and ashamed of her actions. I would have carried those emotions around the rest of the day and probably into the next few days. The defensive Mannette, finding her individual power, would have thrown up her hands while yelling a few choice words at the other person. I would have thought, "You still didn't have to slam on your brakes!" blaming them for causing me stress. I would have remained resentful for at least a few hours or so, blaming the other person for my distress. The older, more tolerant Mannette was able to think, "They seem a little over the top. They must be really struggling with something or have had a bad experience." I remained calm and relaxed throughout the situation. Then I sent good thoughts to the person in the ambulance and the person in front of me, expressing apologies for honking my horn. I moved forward with my day, and the incident didn't even cross my mind again.

This is a great example of our changing perceptions as we grow. Some people choose not to grow. Some people can't even grasp the concept that they might need to grow. Some people are always growing. Can you see yourself in one of the examples above?

Learn to accept that everyone is on their own journey in life, but they may not move at the same speed you do. You want to be tolerant of other's experiences and journeys. This is sometimes what happens in relationships: one of you will be driving the speed limit, and the other one is speeding ahead. The first thing that happens is the one who is behind, gets fearful, and literally feels a distance forming between them and you. This is when we find ourselves saying things to the other person like, "You're acting different," "You're not paying attention to me," or "You don't understand me." It's okay to grow at different speeds as long as you maintain common interest, values, and open communication. As my friend Kate always says, "Let them be them, and you be you."

You Don't Choose Your Family

You don't get to choose your family, but they have more than likely proven who they are and what they are capable of throughout the years. You do choose what behaviors are acceptable for you and all your relationships. Family members don't get special treatment just because they are family, especially if they were or still are abusive. They have to earn your trust and respect just like anyone else you have a relationship with.

One thing to keep in mind is they learned their behaviors from their parents, just like you learned your behaviors from your parents. We are all a product of our environment and have to choose to re-learn certain behaviors as a survivor. I'm not saying you should make excuses for anyone, just accept them for who they are, don't keep waiting for them to change, and set firm boundaries when needed. Let them be them, and you be you.

The Perfect Person for Me

I personally feel that we all choose relationships that teach us lessons about ourselves and the world. You may recognize the same kind of people showing up in your life over and over again until you master whatever it is you need to learn. Ironically, the commonality in each one of your relationships is you. Maybe your lesson is as simple as learning not to be with an abusive person.

Start being more particular about who you spend your time with. Making better choices in terms of whom you associate with, it gets easier as you learn to respect and value yourself. Ask yourself the following questions:

REFLECTIONS:

- Why do I continually have similar people coming and going in my life?
- Why don't my friendships or relationships last?
- What have I learned from my past relationships?
- What kind of people do I want to have in my life going forward?

If you have made bad choices with partners in the past, remember you can make new healthy choices going forward. Choosing a partner is one of the most important decisions you will make in your life, for yourself and your children. You have the privilege of choosing the perfect person for you, and you deserve a wonderful person who respects and values the amazing individual you are.

Why is it that most people seek out a partner in a similar manner to going fishing? What I mean is I know women who accept whatever fish they catch. If you go fishing and catch a trout, but you don't like trout, why would you keep it? Throw it back and keep fishing for salmon, if that is what you like. We each like different things and what you like may not be what your friend likes, so keep fishing until you catch your perfect fish.

Use the questions and list below to create a detailed list of what you really need and want in your relationships going forward. Your list needs to be specific and include characteristics, values, morals, interests, and any other items that are important to you. Consider the choices you have made in the past. What things have and haven't worked in your relationships? Evaluate your relationships and how they have changed throughout the years. Remember always to consider what is best for you and your children.

If you can only think about what you don't want, write it down, then go through your list and beside each negative trait, write down the opposite (positive) trait. If you struggle to recognize positive traits, look up the antonyms for that trait. Some of your answers might be similar. If so, just like before, choose what best describes what you want. What have I learned from my past relationships?

🍃 REFLECTIONS

- What was different in each relationship?
- What was the same in each relationship?
- What did I love about my relationships?

- Are these things still important to me?

- What did I hate about my relationships?

- What healthy qualities do I need and want now?

- What do I not want in a partner?

- What kind of characteristics do I want in a partner?

- Have I ever received unconditional acceptance, love, and respect from a partner?

- How important are these things to me now?

- Have I ever had a loyal partner?

- Have I ever trusted a partner?

Examples of Relationship Desires:

You may want to include activities or interest in your list. (sports, cooking, traveling, music, art, etc.) Fill in the blank with the words you desire from below.

I desire to be	I desire to be with someone
accepted	affectionate
acknowledged	amusing
appreciated	compassionate
celebrated	enthusiastic
championed	fun

content	hopeful
encouraged	joyful
happy	kind
heard	loyal
known	optimistic
loved	peaceful
reassured	supportive
respected	tolerant
trusted	trustworthy

What is Your Perfect Partner Like?

In your *Finding Your Voice* workbook, write down everything you desire in a perfect partner that surfaced throughout this section (traits, qualities, behavior, etc.). Include ten to fifteen items or as many as you can think of, then number them. More is better in this case. Proceed through your list using the Emotional Needs Comparison Exercise method from chapter 6 page 159.

1. Ask yourself the following question. **Which (trait, quality, etc.) can I NOT live without?** Put a checkmark next to the items that are important to you. Remember, some of your answers might be similar. If so, combine those answers into one.

2. Go through each item separately as follows: Compare 1 & 2, 3, 4, 5, 6, 7, 8, 9, 10. Next 2 & 3, 4, etc. Next 3 & 4, 5, etc. Move through this exercise quickly. Don't think about it too much. Listen to your gut and, be honest with yourself.

3. List the items that have the most check marks in order of importance.

4. Now that you have a list, apply the top ten items to the following question:

5. Which items have I experienced in my relationships? When? With whom?

Your next goal is to start focusing more on these items in potential partners going forward. Use this list as your guide for what kind of partner you want to manifest in your life. The top six items are your primary focus, but all ten have a certain amount of values. I would suggest you only accept someone who has at least three of your top six and at least two more of your entire top ten. You aren't going to obtain what you want if you settle for only three items at the bottom of your list. You are worthy of receiving what you desire in your relationships. It is time to recognize you deserve more.

When you learn only to accept relationships that include these items, you have the possibility of developing healthier relationships that fulfill your personal needs and desires. Your desires in a partner may alter or change as you grow and become healthier. You may want to revisit this exercise over the next year as you continue to heal.

After I divorced my first husband, all I knew was what I didn't want anymore. My problem in the beginning was I didn't have any idea of what I wanted. I would literally bring home whatever man I found who gave me attention or made me feel good at the moment. The problem was I just brought home more of the same kind of men and relationships. As time passed, I realized I was just repeating what I knew, and in order to change, I would have to change my intention.

So, I made a list of what I wanted in a partner. It took some time to manifest a positive, healthy partner only because it took time for me to know what I needed and desired in a healthy relationship. I learned to focus on what I wanted and didn't accept anything less for myself. Once I held myself and my relationships to a higher standard, I only allowed healthy people in my life.

My daughter used these methods years ago. She made her list, and within a couple of years, he found her from across the room at a work function. He is nine out of 10 things on her list. Four years later they were happily married in Italy. The key was she knew what she wanted and believed she deserved it.

Parenting Insight

Parenting A Child Who Has Been Abused

If you're parenting a child that has been abused, your role is getting your child help while being supportive, compassionate, and empathetic. Your child – no matter the age – needs professional help sooner rather than later. If your child is an adult, I would advise you to persuade them to seek out a professional that specializes in abuse. Remember, you can't force an adult child to get help, but you can remain supportive as they transition from victim to survivor. They will ultimately have to do the work themselves no matter how much you want to help them. Remain supportive and sympathetic, and hopefully, they will find their way.

If your child is grown and exhibiting destructive behaviors while denying they need help, I feel for you. Either they will eventually ask for the help they need, or they will continue down an unhealthy path. In some cases, you, other family members and their friends may need to try an intervention, but even in this case, they will ultimately accept help or not. Whichever path they take, it isn't your decision.

When it comes to your younger children, you want to get them into therapy as soon as possible. Seek out a professional who specializes in abuse, so they can help your child understand and deal with their experience. Talk to the professional and learn what you can do to support your child through their healing journey. Learn what you can about abuse, how it affects each individual's personality, and the possible changes in behaviors your child may experience. The more you know, the easier it will be for you and them.

Parenting As A Survivor

Your children are the most precious things in your life. I feel abuse survivors have to stop the cycle when it comes to our children and even our grandchildren. I realize parenting isn't easy, but none of us want our children to experience the abuse we experienced.

We each have a choice to protect, nourish, and guide our children no matter what has happened to us. My objective as a parent was to take everything I learned and pass it on to my children. I was an observant mother while empowering my children as individuals. The following are what I consider to be the primary guidelines for raising healthy children, so they don't have to experience the horrific things we did.

Protect Your Child

It's your job to keep your children safe and protect them by pre-qualifying all of your relationships. Don't allow abusive people into your immediate family unit, including extended family and friends. Not everyone is trustworthy, and it's your job to pay attention to people's behaviors and your children's response to others. If your child doesn't like someone, don't force them to accept them, especially young children. Their intuition can be more in tune than ours. Don't set yourself or your children up for abusive situations or relationships.

Teach Your Child to Protect Themselves

My biggest concern for any survivor that becomes a parent is finding balance in your parenting skills. As a survivor, you don't want to overcompensate for your past, but you also don't want to ignore the reality of predators in the world. We have to find a balance between diligent, observational awareness, and not scaring the crap out of our children. Yes, this is a fine line and a vital part to our children not becoming victims.

I feel it's important to have hard conversations with our children from a very young age. We have to explain to them what their private parts are while empowering them to feel comfortable with themselves. They need guidelines and a clear understanding of boundaries when it comes to their bodies. They need to know how valuable their bodies and minds are as well as how to express themselves through emotions, actions, and most of all their voices.

Your child has the ability to protect themselves in most cases with their voice. A voice is a powerful thing, especially when your child feels confident to speak their authentic truth. Your child may not be physically or mentally strong enough to protect themselves from a predator, but their words can set them free. They need always to feel safe speaking the truth, no matter how scary a situation is.

Build an undeniable trust between you and your child that is based on acceptance and respect, so you both have open communication between one another.

1. They need to trust that you will believe and support them, no matter what!

2. They need to know that you are behind them, no matter what a perpetrator says or does!

3. They need to know that you are strong enough to take care of yourself and them, no matter the circumstances or what they have been told.

4. They need to understand they have a powerful voice, especially in confusing, fearful, and uncertain situations. They need to feel free to speak, and you need to be able to listen without criticism, judgment or doubt.

Empower your children with a belief in themselves if you want them to protect themselves and express what they know and how they feel in any situation. Treat your child with respect and acceptance and you will get the same in return. These are the kind of things that build a strong, lasting relationship between you and your child, a relationship free of secrets, uncertainty, and hopefully abuse.

Lead by Example

Lead by example, so your children learn how healthy people participate in relationships and life. Our children learn by watching how we handle ourselves, our relationships, and the world. Your child will mimic whomever and whatever they are exposed to. Demonstrate healthy behaviors and reactions for your children because they are always watching.

Keep in mind: just because you experienced abuse, it doesn't mean your child has to, especially if you heal your past and your pain while improving your relationships with others and your children. You have the capacity to stop the cycle of abuse one family at a time starting with yours.

Note: Enjoy your children and let yourself be a kid, especially if you didn't have a carefree childhood. Have fun, laugh, and play with them. They'll be grown before you know it. Remember, they have wants, needs, and desires that may not be the same as yours. Let them grow up and be the unique individual they are meant to be.

My wish is that you have started cultivating healthier relationships. Like I said at the beginning of this chapter, your relationships with others are similar to the relationship you have with yourself. The only difference is we need to include trust, excellent communication, and healthy boundaries along with unconditional acceptance, love, and respect. Stop, take a look in the mirror and look how far you have come. Remember those baby steps I talked about earlier on? You are now running toward a better life. You are still going to trip and fall occasionally but with less frequency and now you know how to get back up and keep going no matter how big the tumble.

Look at your magnificent grove of trees and how amazing they are. Hopefully, you have gained mutual love, respect, trust, and honest communication in your own relationships. I hope you have a better understanding of what kind of relationships you want to cultivate within your aspen grove.

One-Month Follow-up Questions

I would like you to reflect on the follow-up questions below once a month over the next three months.

How much better are my relationships with my children after one month?

1   2   3   4   5   6   7   8   9   10

How much better is my relationship with my partner after one month?

1   2   3   4   5   6   7   8   9   10

How much better is my relationship with my family after one month?

1   2   3   4   5   6   7   8   9   10

How much better is my relationship with my friends after one month?

1   2   3   4   5   6   7   8   9   10

The Answer

• • • • • • • • • • • • • • • • • • •

*"The gift of healing is mostly about the journey, and the
destination will evolve in time with each step you take."*

R EMEMBER THE POEM BY PATRICK OVERTON, *"When you walk
to the edge of all the light you have and take that first step into
the darkness of the unknown, you must believe that one of two things
will happen. There will be something solid for you to stand upon or
you will be taught to fly."*

I can look back now and see my own journey so clearly. The day
I realized I was metaphorically and literally flying was when I
found myself moving to Singapore for
my husband's career, with my unused
passport in hand. I was sitting in business class when I realized I had manifested this new life for myself full of
new, healthy experiences, adventures,
and people. As I sat in my lounge chair
that I would fold down into a bed a

307

few hours later, I graciously took a warm towel from the flight attendant to clean my hands before she handed me a glass of champagne. Every few minutes another flight attendant would walk by and either offer me a magazine or ask if they could help me in any way. I buckled in for my eighteen-hour flight to the other side of the world where my new life awaited me.

As I sipped my champagne, I thought back to where I started and all the different experiences throughout my life that had brought me to that point and place. As a tear of gratitude and anticipation fell down my cheek, I closed my eyes and gave thanks to God for how far I had come from that small blue and white trailer on the farm where I was just trying to survive.

There were so many times I felt lost, and I didn't know how I was going to take another step, but I always believed in myself and had faith in something bigger. With each step, I became stronger and more confident, the darkness began to dim, and the light started to breakthrough. With each challenge I overcame, the light became brighter. As I focused on the possibilities, my fear subsided. Once the light became bright enough to see clearly, I realized I had wings, and I could fly all along.

At this point, you may have more questions than answers. Hang in there! As you grow and heal everything will become clearer, and you will find yourself becoming more confident with each change you embrace. I don't claim to have all the answers, but I can tell you there is hope, and you **_can_** heal from the pain of your past experiences! You possess the power to defeat and break the cycle of abuse in your life through the understanding you have gained from this book along with changes you have made and will continue to make.

By now you've found your enormously powerful voice!

It took courage for you to take on this book. I am sure it has brought up uncomfortable feelings and memories but more importantly, I hope it has helped you look at your life in a different way. I commend you for the work you have done up until now, and the work you will continue to do! I realize these exercises were not simple or easy. I asked a LOT from you in these pages, and you continually rose to the occasion! Look at how far you have come! You should be so proud of yourself.

I'm proud of you for taking a chance on yourself, stepping out of denial, and facing your past and all the pain that comes with it. I wish I could've have been there with you physically, holding your hand and being a shoulder to cry on as you learned how to accept, love, and respect yourself unconditionally. I wish I could've been standing beside you speaking affirmation while encouraging you directly until you believed every word! Look at you now; you have walked through the process of building yourself up while finding your own strength and power. I bet your affirmations have become empowering statements of self-confidence and self-assurance.

You have pushed through confronting your survivor skills while recognizing they have been your safety net and your barriers for so long. I know firsthand how challenging those survival skills are to change and overcome, but I'm sure you are conquering them! You will continue discovering more about yourself as you change and evolve. You are reaching for your dreams and your desires.

Can you see your desires taking shape and manifesting before your own eyes? I wish I was there to see it firsthand!

I'm sure you are taking advantage of the positive power of the Happy Boosters as you have implemented them into your life. I know you are taming those Happy Busters as you learn to keep them in check. I truly hope your story of abuse is resting quietly in your past where it belongs! I hope you have forgiven yourself wholeheartedly for any past indiscretion or false beliefs.

I hope you start to see your relationships changing for the better! You may even begin acquiring a few new healthy ones along the way. If you haven't yet, I truly believe you're well on your way and have all the tools you need to pick the right people to surround yourself with. I trust your communication skills have improved, and you have healthy boundaries in place to build a strong foundation with others. Keep reaching for your dreams as you continue your personal healing journey. You are courageous. You deserve happiness and a life full of love and joy!

What are you waiting for? It's time for you to fly and live the life you dare to dream of. You can do this! You have everything you need within yourself to change your life for the better!

"Be the person you want to be tomorrow, today!"

I am honored you chose me to assist you on this journey of healing.

    Thank you,
    Mannette

About the Author

MANNETTE MORGAN IS A CERTIFIED life coach from the Academy of Solution Focus Training, completed 2010 and American University of NLP completed 2012.

Mannette has led motivational self-improvement classes and workshops at several organizations since 2013 including Dress for Success of Denver, Warren Village, Warren Village First Step and Women's Bean Project of Denver. All of these organizations help women that are struggling, in need of support, guidance, and training. A few of the topics taught include *How to Heal after Abuse, Overcoming Anxiety and Stress, Finding more Happiness, Understanding and Improving Relationships, Parenting After Abuse,* and overall self-improvement. Mannette's classes ranged from one and a half hours to four hours and multiple classes over constitutive months.

Mannette has also led group workshops for women seeking self-improvement since 2012 and women's weekend mountain retreats that have inspired, rejuvenated and encouraged self-improvement for women seeking balance and inspiration.

She has professionally coached individual victims and survivors of abuse since 2010, helping them improve, change, and recover from the effects of abuse. Clients have gained a true understanding of how abuse has affected their lives while learning self-respect, strength, self-confidence, and how to live a healthier, happier life.

Reference

All is Well Heal Your Body with Medicine, Affirmations, and Intuition; authors, Louise Hay and Mona Lisa Schulz M.D., PH.D
Publisher Hay House, March 2013, May 2014

Better than Before What I learned about making and breaking habits -to sleep more, quit sugar, procrastinate less, and generally build a happier life; author Gritchen Rubin
Publisher Broadway Books, 2015

The Courage to Heal, A guide for Women Survivors of child Sexual Abuse; authors Ellen Bass & Laura Davis and
The first edition of this book was published in 1988 by Harper & Row, Publishers.

Happy For No Reason 7 Steps to Being Happy from the Inside Out; authors Marci Shimoff and Carol Kine
Publisher Free Press, 2008

The 5 Love Languages The Secret to Love That Last; author, Gary Chapman
Northfield Publishing, 1992, 1995,2004, 2010

The 5 Love Language of Children; authors Gary Chapman and Ross Campbell
Northfield Publishing, 1997, 2005, 2012